Ultimate
Questions

Ultimate Questions

Nathaniel Micklem

ABINGDON PRESS

NEW YORK • NASHVILLE

ULTIMATE QUESTIONS

Copyright MCMLV by Pierce & Washabaugh

Library of Congress Catalog Card Number: 55-5054

SET UP, PRINTED, AND BOUND BY THE
PARTHENON PRESS, AT NASHVILLE,
TENNESSEE, UNITED STATES OF AMERICA

Preface

    I have long puzzled over the proper title for this book. I have hit upon several appropriate but improper titles, such as "The Last Thoughts of a Discontented Theologian," or "The Regrettable Bankruptcy of Traditional Theology," or even, least satisfactory but most appropriate, "Who Was This Man?" For, as I see it, the real theme of the book, after a preliminary uncluttering, is the inescapable question put to the modern, serious, educated man by the enigmatic figure of Jesus of Nazareth, as I understand sober historical inquiry to present him to our consideration. I surmise that the varying forms of orthodoxy, each after its kind, will be shocked at much that I have written. In shocking them I take no pleasure. But after many long years given to religious and theological study I understand so well why many serious and not irreligious minds are alienated from the Christian faith. The Christian tradition of doctrine as popularly understood, and indeed as not infrequently expounded by its learned sponsors, seems to me to be largely pre-Copernican in outlook. I have no new system to offer in its stead, but I would make my appeal to candid and religious minds who are offended by traditional presentations to consider afresh whether in the light of history we may not regard the great symbols of the Christian tradition as pointing to those last secrets which may only be apprehended, and that imperfectly, by faith.

These chapters had a kind of trial trip or maiden voyage when a few years ago I was required by the Student Christian Movement to theologize on five consecutive mornings before a somewhat formidable collection of university teachers from various faculties in Great Britain. For the purposes of the Cole Lectures, delivered at Vanderbilt University in the spring of 1954, my discourses were rewritten, extended, and revised. They are better than they were. I could wish them better still.

I distinguish quite clearly in my own mind between lectures and a book. The difference lies in style rather than in substance. A lecture is written to be spoken. The lecturer has an audience in view; his lecture should be an exercise in rhetoric. By this I do not mean that it should be rhetorical in the vulgar sense; I mean that sentences which in a speech would be admirable may seem out of place in a literary composition. In the following pages the reader is offered the Cole Lectures substantially as they were delivered.

Rereading the lectures in book form will remind me of one of the happiest experiences of my life, when for a few months it was my privilege to serve on the teaching staff of Vanderbilt University, amid the generous, kindly, gracious people of the South. I may mention here the names of Dr. Harvie Branscomb, chancellor of the university, and Dr. J. K. Benton, dean of the School of Religion, but how many more names do I mention privately and gratefully!

NATHANIEL MICKLEM

Contents

I
The Language of
Religion

It would seem that three religions or quasi religions strive for the soul of modern man. There is Humanism, there is Marxism, and there is Christianity, and all three should be treated with respect. Humanism is the somewhat wistful religion of men of culture, who inherit and value the spiritual traditions of the West, but who no longer find credible the dogmatic assertions of the Christian creeds. Marxism claims, indeed, to be an irreligion rather than a religion; it is atheist in profession; it wages war against all pretensions of the transcendental; it avoids religious language, but it offers men a complete philosophy of life like a great religion; it kindles hope and faith and comes to men like a revelation, and if its conception of "matter" is analyzed, it will be found to be far removed from the crude materialism of Haeckel and the materialists of the nineteenth century; it is a form of immanence philosophy, which in spite of its dynamic quality and its preoccupation with history and economics, sometimes reminds us of the philosophy of Spinoza, the "God-intoxicated" man. Christianity is hard to define. The sensitive are apt to contrast "ideal" or "real" or "true" Christianity with actual or empirical Christianity.

11

What ideal or pure Christianity might be I cannot say, for most men mean by the phrase nothing but Christianity as they wish it were. As for empirical Christianity, though it is doubtless a great power for good in the world, and though here and there it shows remarkable signs of life, and has even in very recent years revealed unsuspected power and heroism, yet it is quite plain that "the churches" are not offering to the world a form of religion which kindles conviction or enthusiasm in the minds of the typical "modern man," whether of the universities or of the factories, and that it is not in general approving itself as answering the needs, the questions, the agonies of the present time.

With the religiously minded men who today are alienated from Christianity as represented by the churches I have great sympathy. I often find myself nearer to them than to those Christians who claim to have all the answers, who repeat the stupendous assertions of the traditional faith as if they were scientific propositions, and who take "the gospel" very much for granted. I could wish a considerable infiltration of agnosticism into the ecclesiastics and the dogmatists. I believe, however, that some form of Christianity, or some religion that derives from historical Christianity and feeds upon the great Christian symbols, will alone meet the intellectual needs and the practical exigencies of the present time. Hence I address myself primarily to those Christians who, still claiming to be Christians, are much perplexed, and to those who would hesitate to call themselves Christians but are open to consider the claims of Christianity if only these are set before them in intelligible terms.

It will be convenient if I make plain from the beginning my own personal attitude to the old creeds, confessions, and theologies of traditional Christianity. I have no

12

startling new "heresy" to propound; I have no "systematic theology" to offer in the place of older theories; I have no proofs that Christianity is true; but, as Father Tyrrell said, the world can never get away from "that strange Man upon his cross," and I regard the great theologies and confessions of the past as a vast portrait gallery, where the paintings by various artists are all of the selfsame Person. The artists belong to many generations. They think the thoughts, they use the idiom, each of his own age. Origen and Irenaeus, Augustine of Hippo and John of Damascus, Thomas Aquinas and Bonaventura, Luther and Calvin, Jonathan Edwards and Horace Bushnell, Schleiermacher and Karl Barth—how they differ among themselves if we consider technically their various propositions! Yet each of them has painted Christ as he sees him. Not all the portraits are equally good, but all are recognizable; nor need we doubt that if we have time to study all these portraits, we shall know more of Christ than if we pay attention to one only. Therefore for myself I would say that I accept and I reject all these old statements. I accept them because they offer recognizable portraits of Christ. I reject them because none can be hailed as final or fully satisfactory for our present age. I certainly shall not attempt a new portrait of my own. That would be a task altogether beyond my powers. I shall regard myself as a man of this century set down in this great portrait gallery and permitted in this setting to put down some of his thoughts.

Where, then, shall I start? From the Bible or from reason? If we are persons of intellectual integrity, and at the same time of due intellectual humility, we must avoid obscurantism or mere credulity on the one side and a merely arid rationalism upon the other. As we are of intellectual integrity, we cannot accept religious truths on the authority of someone else. As we are of intellectual humility, we cannot suppose that there is no truth except such as we may derive from the process of our syllogisms.

At least it is plain that for present purposes the Bible is no proper starting point, and this for several reasons. First, because I cannot here discuss, still less decide, the limits of the canon; second, because the interpretation of the Bible is no simple matter; and third, because if I started from the Bible as authoritative, I should not carry with me those whom I would more particularly address.

But if I say that I shall start from reason, I must guard against a likely misunderstanding; for reason in these days is often identified with man's faculty of ratiocination and the processes of correct thinking, with logic, in fact. But reason has traditionally a wider connotation. It stands for man's rational endowment whereby he takes first principles for self-evident, as, for instance, that contradictories cannot be simultaneously true of the same subject, or that every event must have an adequate cause, or that to do right is right. No reasoning is possible except upon the basis of some presuppositions accepted by both parties to the argument. This is as true of scientific thinking as of religious thinking. Scientific reasoning, for instance, is impossible with anyone who will not agree that the universe is a rational system, or who maintains that all sensible experience is part of life's great illusion. I cannot find any starting point that will not involve some assumptions that may be questioned.

But I fall back upon the good sense of a person who has played a much larger part heretofore in jurisprudence than in theology, I mean "the reasonable man." In American courts, as in British courts also, there often occur cases where, that a just decision be reached in a matter, let us say of negligence, it is necessary for the judge or the jury to decide what "the reasonable man" might be supposed to have done under the given circumstances. This

14

is an issue where no precision is possible. Yet in general terms we know and agree as to what conduct is reasonable as opposed to criminally careless. My appeal in theology is to this same "reasonable man" in another aspect of his putative being. I shall only ask you to grant what, as I suppose, the "reasonable man" might well be willing to admit; and I shall take for my text, if text may be allowed me, "I will hear what God the Lord will speak." I shall thus assume what I cannot prove, that God is, and that man in some manner and in some degree may be aware of him. I am sure that for my purposes I may be granted that.

In my attempt to pierce the mists which surround man's mortal life I would close my eyes to no fact which may be presented to me; I would close my ears to no voice from which I may perhaps learn anything to my advantage; as I face life with such integrity as may be given me, "I will hear what God the Lord will speak"— to me. This may suggest that my approach to these great issues will be entirely subjective, individualistic, and miserably limited to my own poor ideas. But do not forget that I conceive myself to be standing in that great picture gallery; I am not limited to my own small experience. I will hear what God the Lord may seem to have said to Augustine and Thomas and Schleiermacher; yes, and to Plato and Virgil, but I shall not give my full consent unless I at least dimly see that which these great men claim to have seen, unless there is an answer in my own heart to what I hear through them. Wrote the poet George Wither:

> If she be not so to me,
> what care I how fair she be? [1]

[1] "The Lover's Resolution."

15

I can tell you only what I, as I have looked and listened, seem to have seen and heard.

I certainly shall not assume in advance that God has spoken to mankind only through the Bible and the Christian Fathers. I will hear, that is, I desire to hear, what God the Lord will say to me through nature and through art, through science and through secular history, through the common experiences of life as I meet it from day to day, through the loyalties and sanctities of home and friendship, through Socrates and through Shelley, through Marx and through Einstein, as well as through the Bible and through the historic figure of Jesus Christ. I dare not, a priori or on principle, refuse to listen to what may be said outside the distinctively Christian faith. And what mental perturbation, what schizophrenia, as I believe psychologists call it, would arise in me if I should find that what I seemed to learn and hear through the Christian witness should contradict what I learned from the rest of life and history!

It is claimed by many that the Bible, or at least Jesus Christ, has an authority to which all other supposed revelations must submit, and by which they must be judged. We must then raise, at least in passing, the question of the nature of authority in the field of religion. Life knows many authorities. There is the authority of parents to which we were subject when we were children; there is the authority of the schoolteacher; there is the authority of the law, the authority of specialists, the authority of conscience. Is authority in religion comparable to any one of these? It is often supposed that authority in religion is like the authority of parents. "Mother knows best" is generally a statement of fact and is at any rate a proper expression of authority. "The good Book" tells you to do this or that, therefore be a good boy and obey; Mother Church or the Holy Father tells you, and he knows best

—how familiar we are with this type of exhortation! And we are the more drawn to this kind of authority the more feelingly we are aware that we are but children, ignorant, weak, and in sore need of direction. But such an authority is not satisfactory in religion, if indeed it has any place in religion at all. For parental authority is that out of which we grow as we develop into manhood. We can hardly pay too much attention to "the good Book," but, after all, the devil's ability to cite Scripture for his own purposes is quite proverbial, and Mother Church and the Holy Father often ask us to believe things which appear on mature reflection to be in the highest degree improbable. Moreover, the Bible bids us love the Lord our God with all our mind, and we cannot reasonably suppose that in religion it is our duty to obey and not to think. "Theirs not to reason why" may belong to the good life of the soldier in battle but not to the full life of religion. If we like to say that the only final authority in religion is the truth or God himself, we shall have glimpsed the obvious but gone no way to illumine our problem. How are we to know the mind of God? Before men brought up in the modern scientific, individualistic, skeptical age it may be unnecessary to plead that in religion there can be no infallible authorities on earth. It may be more important to insist that the child is not to be commended for wisdom who despises "what Mother says" or "what our schoolmaster teaches," and that serious people respect the principles of the law and the findings, however tentative, of the specialists. When

> John P. Robinson, he
> Sez they didn't know everythin' down in Judee,[2]

he was quite right, but they knew very much "down

[2] James Russell Lowell, *The Biglow Papers*, Ser. 1., No. 3.

in Judee" to which he would have been well advised to pay attention. There is an extreme frivolity about the attitude of many modern men who, presented with the most serious issues of life, the ultimate questions of the nature and destiny of man, are content to reject, neglect, pour scorn upon the accumulated wisdom of mankind. They resemble the astronomer who denied the existence of God on the ground that having swept the skies with his telescope, he had observed no trace of him. Intellectual integrity must go with intellectual humility.

It will be urged by some that the authority of Jesus Christ is absolute. I am not interested to deny that in principle, but in any particular case we cannot make practical application of this principle until we are sure that we know exactly what he said, that we correctly understand it, and that we are capable without error of applying it to our twentieth-century questions. It is of the nature and essence of spiritual authority that it appeals to reason and to insight. Jesus Christ never asked men to follow him blindfold. He said, "Take heed then how ye hear." God speaks to us through the Bible, not because we can look up, as in an encyclopedia, what he has said, but because, as we read and meditate upon the Bible, he speaks to us directly through it. He speaks to us through the words of Jesus Christ, but we cannot without thinking apply these words to our immediate questions. We are given a compass, not a map. So much for authority.

Let us consider "the Christian faith," "the Christian revelation." What are we to understand by "revelation"? This is not a distinctively Christian question. God is not a Something that can be studied in the natural sciences. It is true that when we pass from physics to metaphysics, we may be driven to the hypothesis that there must be a First Cause, an Absolute, a Supreme Mind. But when

18

we look out over the spiritual history of mankind, it is very plain that men have not worshiped and offered prayer and sacrifice to some hypothesis; they have lived by faith; they have believed that the mysterious Power or Powers behind phenomena have in some way made themselves known to us. We as rational modern men may be very sure that if God has really spoken to animists and devil worshipers and witch doctors, what he has said must have been very grievously misheard; we may conclude, indeed, that very much that passes for religion in history and at the present day has in reality nothing to do with religion at all; it is illusion, neurosis, nonsense. But as people who, however dimly and intermittently, are aware of God, we cannot believe that God has left mankind wholly without witness to himself. Yet if God be in any degree known, it can be only because he has revealed himself, and how could anyone who has studied the prayers of primitive peoples or read the *Apology* of Plato or the *Hymn to Zeus* of Cleanthes suppose that God has revealed himself only to Christians and in earlier days to Jews? Revelation is a human question, not merely a Christian question.

But what is the nature of revelation? What is that which has been revealed? The traditional Christian answer is familiar. It is to the effect that God has no doubt spoken to man in many ages and in many religions through nature, through reason, through conscience, through mystical experience; this is the sphere of "natural religion"; but he has fully and completely revealed himself in Jesus Christ, and this supernatural revelation may be summed up in the great doctrines of the Church, the Trinity, the Incarnation, the Atonement, and the like.

But there are grave difficulties in this view. If Zoroaster or Ikhnaton or Socrates or Virgil was really aware of

19

God, that is, to change the phraseology, if God really spoke to them, I can see nothing less supernatural about that than his speaking to Jeremiah or to Paul. It is replied that the Bible proclaims saving truths which God did not reveal to the world outside the Bible. Here it is presupposed that revelation comes in the form of "truths." At this point, I am sure, we must take issue with traditional ideas. I am not denying that the great Christian doctrines point to the truth, but propositions such as theological statements are not revealed from heaven, and if they were, they would of necessity be distorted in any possible human language. They arise out of man's intellectual travail. In revelation it is God who reveals, and it is God who is revealed. Revelation is not doctrine.

Our modern danger, our Protestant danger, is to over-intellectualize religion. It is not to man's intellect alone that God reveals himself. I imagine you climbing with a friend in a strange part of the country. You have plodded on through the woods and then among the dark crevasses, and then quite suddenly and quite unexpectedly you emerge upon a ledge or plateau in the open. The ground falls away before your feet, and spread out before you expands a panorama of sky and cloud and mountains and streams, and below you in the distance the quiet fields and the sea beyond. And you just gasp. For a minute or two neither of you says a word; then gradually you point to this or that; the scene begins to sort itself out in your mind; you commit it to memory; you will be able to describe it to people when you get home—yet you never will be able to describe it; it baffles all power and range of words. I offer this as a real parallel to what is revelation. In the first moment of wonder, when the glory of the scene breaks upon heart and mind, there is, no doubt, an intellectual element, but it is

20

secondary; it becomes predominant only when you try to analyze, to remember, to report. The doctrines of the Christian faith, the so-called "truths of revelation," are the agreed statements, or the more or less agreed statements, the very imperfect statements, of those who are trying to express what it means to see the glory of God in the face of Jesus Christ. The "truths" are not the revelation; they only point to it, and except in so far as they effectively point to it, they are useless to us or misleading. Perhaps Christian teachers should not be so cast down and troubled at the unbelief of the modern world. These doctrines which they so persuasively expound may be technically good descriptions of the spiritual scene, but if they do not evoke in others a sense of the wonder and the glory they are meant to express, they cannot come as revelation. Christian teachers, it may be, must learn to paint in another style or use another medium.

We do wrong to suppose that the Christian revelation can be expressed only in doctrines and in words. We are trained in the use of words; our natural medium of expression is through words and intellectual concepts, and it may well be that words are the best mediums for the expression of religious revelation. But certainly they are not the only ones, and there are many to whom they are not the first and most natural. I point you to three men, each of whom has seen something of the glory of God in the coming of Jesus Christ. Here is Milton— he writes "On the Morning of Christ's Nativity"; here is Botticelli—he paints "The Supplication Dance of the Shepherds"; here is Bach—he composes the *Christmas Oratorio*. There are those to whom Botticelli or Bach really conveys something of the glory seen, to whom the splendid language of Milton means nothing, and our learned treatises on the Incarnation mean less than nothing.

I well remember how one of my sons, when he was very young, came one sunny morning into my dressing room, and looking out of the window, saw the may and the laburnum and the guelder-roses all in bloom, as if they had burst suddenly into flower. And he said, "I must sing to it." That has always seemed to me exactly the right response. Somewhere in the *Colloquia Peripatetica* the Rabbi Duncan, A. B. Davidson's predecessor in the chair of Hebrew in Edinburgh, writes, "When I knew that there was a God, I danced upon the Brig o' Dee with delight." In that picture by Botticelli to which I referred just now the angels are seen dancing in a ring above the "cratch of brute beasts" where the infant Jesus lies. And is not Christ present in the basilica built for Christian worship? What more natural, then, than that in the early days of the Church's history the faithful should join hands in the church below at the time of sacred worship and consciously join in the dance of the angels in heaven? Let us remember that poetry and music and the dance are nearer to revelation than is doctrinal statement. Our faith rests in God, not in the propositions of the theologians. We may even venture the opinion that doctrinal statement divorced from music, song, and dance is dead.

It is often assumed that if on any subject I make an accurate statement, I have certainly conveyed the truth to you. That is a mistake. The words of a speaker may be accurate, but if the hearer cannot understand them, or understands them amiss, the truth has not been conveyed to him. The words of our traditional creeds may be quite accurate, but unless they evoke in the hearer a response of heart and mind to that which they assert, there is no revelation. If you say to a man on Easter,

"Christ the Lord is risen today," and he drawls back,
"Oh, really?" he has not understood or believed, even
though he accepts your statement without question.
If when you say "Christ the Lord is risen today," he
responds with "Hallelujah!" it is possible that he has
understood. We can put this in current language by
saying that the assertions of the Christian faith are
"existential." That is to say, they are not addressed to the
intellect alone but to the whole person; they are not
understood if there is merely an intellectual response to
them; there must be a total response of the whole personality, mind, heart, and will; only so are they lifted into
the sphere of revelation.

I hope I have sufficiently elaborated and made
clear this point. We must be concerned with the verbal
expression of revelation and with the significance of the
Christian faith for our thought as men of the modern
age. That is as it should be, but it is well for us always
to bear in mind that religion or religious truth is not of
the intellect alone.

I come back, then, to this phrase "the truths of religion." What sort of truths are these? It is for theological thinking of the first importance to realize that
truths are of very different kinds. There is, for instance,
the truth, or the alleged truth (for I stumbled at pons
asinorum), that the angles at the base of an isosceles
triangle are equal, and that if the equal sides are produced, the exterior angles will be also equal. Whether or
not this is really true you must ask Einstein; but even
Einstein, as I suppose, would agree that two and two
make four or something very like it. Such are the truths
of mathematics. Then there are the truths of science.
Truth here, I think, means accuracy. If you understand
the definition of the terms of a scientific statement, and
the facts are correct, the whole truth, so far as the facts

23

are concerned, has been conveyed to you in the proposition; there is no penumbra of obscurity; there are no overtones. Then again there is such a proposition as, "I dislike this book very much." That, I hope, is not yet a truth, but such it may become; it is not, however, a statement with which the natural sciences can deal, for it cannot be tested with any accuracy by any of the methods of science—unless indeed your dislike should attain the pitch of nausea; it is a personal and private truth, if it be true; for no other man can affirm or contradict it from his own personal knowledge. Then there is the truth of the poet who sings that his love "is like a red, red rose." His love can be seen when she walks abroad, and any botanist will affirm that she is easily distinguishable from any rose recorded in the catalogues. Yet we should not do well to call the poet a liar on that account; for he is trying to express what he has seen, and he can convey his apprehension only by a symbol. His we may call symbolic truth. Does religious truth belong to any of these types?

The doctrine of the Holy Trinity is not a mathematical conundrum, and I need not argue that religious truth is not to be identified with mathematical truth. Neither is religious truth mere personal or private truth, for it is concerned with God, and propositions about God must be false or true for all men everywhere. But it seems to be assumed by many Christians and by most unbelievers that Christian doctrine claims to be scientific truth. No wonder, then, that unbelievers have been able to make much easy fun at the expense of the Christian faith. How could God have a Son, they say, and fancy supposing that Jesus Christ reached heaven by ascending in a bee-line above a certain point in Palestine! That is all very silly, but I am afraid that theologians have afforded excuse for this kind of misrepresentation. Most are now

24

ready to admit that there is a figurative element in some of the propositions of the creed, but as to the limits of the figurative there is still no agreement. Most of the heresy hunts (how many and bitter they have been!) have rested implicitly on the assumption that the orthodox formula is a scientifically accurate proposition, so that any other proposition out of harmony with it must be false. Scientific propositions are either accurate or inaccurate; their terms can be exactly defined; they say precisely what they mean, neither more nor less; there is no mystery about them. But the language of religion cannot be like this. Religion is concerned with the mystery of God: we look out upon nature which the sciences study and

> Lo, these are but the outskirts of his ways;
> And how small a whisper do we hear of him!
> But the thunder of his power who can understand?
>
> (A.S.V.)

We can use only human language to speak of God; hence our religious speech must be metaphorical, symbolic, analogical. The truths of religion, therefore, are more like the truths of poetry than like the truths of science.

Such an admission causes anxiety to some religious minds, for there is a popular notion that what the scientists say is true, and that what the poets say is but half true at the best. This is a mistake. The scientific astronomer has much of importance to tell us about the stars; he will explain to us how far away they are, of what they are composed, how old they are, what they weigh, and how fast they travel. His instruction we gratefully receive. The poet who wrote, "When I consider thy heavens, the work of thy fingers, the moon and the stars, which thou hast ordained," was quite ignorant of all the facts of modern astronomy, but he is telling us that God made the stars, and it is his will that they obey. These facts, if they be true, are certainly not secondary truths. We may properly say that to the poet are revealed deeper, more important truths than anything to be learned by looking through a telescope. That God created the heavens and the earth is primary. We must admit at the same time, however, that the idea of creation is a name or symbol for a great mystery which we cannot imagine, and that the "will" of God is an analogy taken from the will of human beings. The poet's truths, deeper and more important though they be than the scientific truths, are not themselves scientifically true. Scientific truths are such in so far as they are accurate; they are never true in the sense of telling us the whole truth about their subject. Every object that falls within the scope of science has, for instance, an aesthetic aspect with which the natural sciences cannot deal at all. No one should dispute what Baedeker says about Mont Blanc, but Shelley and Coleridge have much to say about the mountain which no guidebook and no scientific textbook can reveal. The poets are concerned with truth, with the interpretation of the real and actual world; they are the seers; perhaps we may be allowed to say that the sphere of science is out-sight and that of poetry is in-sight. We can dispense with neither. Here obviously religion is more akin to poetry than to science, and you will not suppose that when I claim that religious truth is more like the truth of poetry than the truth of the natural sciences, I am suggesting that religious truth is an inferior brand of truth.

Religion and poetry are akin, and I think we might say that some forms of religion such as the religion of

26

Ikhnaton, of Plato, of Aristotle, of Spinoza, or of Hegel, are a special kind of poetry. But the traditional Christian religion with Judaism is not a special kind of poetry. It is tied, as poetry is not, to history. When we assert, for instance, that "Christ died for our sins," we are, or we claim to be, asserting a fact, not a poetical truth. Yet certainly it is not, as stated, a scientific fact in the sense of a fact with which the natural sciences can deal. It is not even a fact with which the historian as such can deal. It is, so to put it, a fact of insight, not of demonstration; it is, in intention at least, not a value attached to a historical fact; it is itself, or is alleged to be, a simple fact. Christians are asserting a reality which they see or dimly see; but they do not see it as the inevitable conclusion of a syllogism or as the result of scientific or historical inquiry.

Let us look a little more closely at this statement that Christ died for our sins, or for the sins of the whole world. What does it mean? The answer, I think, is that the words bear no precise meaning at all. To the vast majority of mankind which has given the matter no consideration, I suppose the words are wholly without meaning; they are as meaningless as would be the assertion that Julius Caesar was murdered that we might all have television sets. To many Christians, on the other hand, these words have a very precise meaning; they will explain to us with enthusiasm and full logical consistency the divine "plan of salvation" as they understand it, and will explain exactly how the death of Christ fits into this. There is really no mystery; they understand it all; they "have it all taped," to use a modern phrase. Unhappily, Christians are not unanimous on many important points, and some of the theories they propound are open to the most serious objection on moral or philosophical

27

or theological grounds, and all these theories are, to be frank, just theories. Some of them no doubt manifest deep insights, and none is to be smiled at; but the fact asserted, that Christ died for our sins, which all Christians assert, is to be clearly distinguished from all the many theories about it. What, then, is the fact? I think we must reply that the statement, which bears no precise meaning, points to a profound insight that there is some connection between the sin of mankind in which we all participate and the death of Christ upon the cross, and that there is some connection between his death and the forgiveness of our sins. A statement which bears no precise meaning is not for that reason void.

Religion is concerned both with this world and with the infinite, and with this world as it participates in or reflects or points to the infinite and the eternal. It deals in concepts, intimations, visions that "break through language and escape." Our ordinary, human, workaday language does not reach to God, yet we must speak of God. Thus we speak of God as willing or thinking or feeling; for how can we speak of a personal God at all except in such terms as these? But we should remember that our willing presupposes an overcoming of obstacles, our thinking is discursive, moving laboriously from point to point, our feelings are related to our human passions; only analogically, therefore, can these terms be applied to God. Such terms are necessary to our thought, but they can be true only in some more eminent sense beyond our understanding. How often have we heard ministers and others tell us so glibly what God wants or what God hopes or what God wishes or what God is saying or what God is doing, till we could cry out in insupportable distress, "Sir, thou hast nothing to draw with, and the well is deep." There are theologians of the

28

present generation who in their reaction from the in-
trepid familiarities of popular piety have declared that
God is "the wholly Other." But were he in fact wholly
Other, it would seem that we could not speak about him
at all, or even attach any meaning to the word "God"
itself. That would reduce religion to silence and vacuity.
But it is a question whether any term can be applied to
God and to man in precisely the same sense. Thomas
Aquinas held that all our statements with reference to
God must be analogical; Duns Scotus sought to correct
him by claiming that being as opposed to not-being
is asserted of God and man in the same sense; yet even
this has been denied by Paul Tillich.

Into these subtleties we need not enter. Enough that
the language of religion is analogical and symbolical,
not scientific. If we speak of God, blessed be he, as personal, or of Christ as the Son of God, we must mean
that there is in God that which is analogous to personality in us, and that Christ stands to God in a relationship somehow analogous to that of a human son to a
human father. Where the language of religion is not
analogical, it is symbolical; the Bible and theology are
full of tremendous symbols such as heaven and hell and
the kingdom of God, the fall of man, and the Incarnation. We must understand them as best we can; we may
apprehend them by religious insight; we cannot comprehend them and reduce them to prosaic definition. You
may feel that I am laboring an obvious point, but it
would be hard to exaggerate the amount of misunderstanding, of obscurantism, of heresy-hunting, of spiritual
pride that has arisen from failure to grasp this point.
We must understand the nature of religious language
before we attempt to discuss religious doctrine.

I must indicate one more point of terminology. There

29

is a technical distinction between a legend and a myth. A legend is a story of what men are alleged to have done. A myth is a story of what God or the gods have done. "Myth" is the English form of the Greek word meaning "story." When we say that an event is "mythical," we mean that it did not really happen. In this sense, of course, as Christians believe, the gospel is not mythical. But in the technical sense the gospel is a myth in the sense of being a story of what God has done. I do not wish to suggest that all the myths of antiquity or of the present day are wholly false, but they are not true stories, whereas Christians believe that the gospel is a true story; it is, to use von Harnack's phrase, "the myth come true." But I think it well to lay stress on the word "myth" in this connection because, as a particular instance of what I have said about analogy, it is of much significance for Christian thought. The Bible relates how God called Abraham, empowered Moses, gave the law, sent his prophets; in the last days he spoke by his Son, sent his Son, came in the person of his Son; it tells how the Son of God came down from heaven, lived a man among men, died, rose again, ascended to heaven, where he now sits at the right hand of God; how he sent his Spirit, how he acts in providence and grace. We should not be in the least surprised that all this story sounds incredible to the modern man with his scientific upbringing, a fairy story. This story is often accepted by Christians as a matter of course, a plain tale of intelligible fact; and where it is so accepted as a matter of course, it may well be that the agnostic scientist is far more religious than the Christian. For the scientist is, or he may be, conscious of the immeasurable mystery that surrounds our human life and the physical universe of which he is aware. The true scientist is not so fond as to suppose that science can answer every question; he has, it may be, a profound sense of awe and wonder as he contemplates the unimaginable Being, the supreme Mind, the Infinite, of which we are aware through the transcient and the small. He is not irreligious; but the Christian story of the Saviour from heaven, of the divine Son of God, of the incarnate Word, of

> Our God contracted to a span
> Incomprehensibly made man,

seems to him just a myth. In this sense he is right that the gospel inevitably is mythological in form. It may be doubted whether any Christian can really believe the gospel unless he feels how incredible, how impossible, how beyond all comprehension it really is.

It ill becomes us to suppose that we understand the gospel, that we know all about it, that it is a series of events with which we can deal as we deal with any other facts of history or of science. Yet if God be the living God, if there be any communication between man and God, if God in any degree makes himself known to man, this can be expressed only in terms of story—God spoke, he sent, he came. The language of myth is the only possible language that we can use. Such language cannot be exact and trim and scientific. Yet when we have glimpsed the glory of God in the face of Jesus Christ, and try to express in language that which we have seen, we are bound to tell this story of the speaking, of the sending, of the coming of God himself. It is the language of symbolism and of myth, if you will, but it points to the truth, it expresses the truth, it represents the truth that we have seen. A pedant, a man with no religious insight, a mere literalist may cavil at every phrase, and his comments may at a certain level be fully justified. But when he has seen what we believe that we have seen, he will realize that there is no other language in which the truth can be expressed. The literalist who sees only the words and cannot grasp that which the words are strained to express, and the ecclesiastic who supposes that the whole truth is comprised and adequately defined in the formula which he favors, these alike fail to understand the nature and the language of religion.

We may properly speak of "truths of revelation," and these may, and indeed must, be elongated into doctrines. But the doctrines themselves are never the revelation; they can but point to it. Not only are the Christian doctrines of the Trinity, of the Incarnation, and of the Atonement not themselves the revelation, but except in so far as they are related to Jesus Christ there is nothing essentially distinctive of Christianity in them. The doctrine of the Trinity in its formal aspect is in general a doctrine that Almighty God is personal; that is a doctrine any theist might accept. Our doctrines of the deity of Chirst might, I suppose, be acceptable with another application wherever men have asserted or expected the coming of a divine-human figure; that which is distinctive of the doctrine is its application to Jesus Christ. Other religions might accept our doctrines of the Atonement; it is the reference to Jesus that makes these doctrines Christian. Perhaps I should take a simpler and clearer instance. The doctrine of the fatherhood of God may be called a fundamental doctrine of the Christian faith, but it is not in form a distinctively Christian doctrine. Men spoke of God as Father before the dawn of history; the title Zeus Pater in Greek, Jupiter in Latin, Dyaus Pitar in Sanskrit points to a common doctrine of God's fatherhood prior to the time when the Aryan peoples went their separate ways. That which is distinctive in the Christian doctrine of the fatherhood of God does not lie in the words or the formal doctrine but in the new light, the new depth, the new wonder, the new glory which the doctrine attains when it is connected with the revelation that comes through Jesus Christ. How pale and ghostly does the primitive doctrine of our forefathers seem, who yet glimpsed by revelation something of God's fatherhood, when we compare their experience and confidence with that of those who declare, "God hath sent forth the Spirit of his Son into our hearts, crying, Abba, Father." Am I making clear my point that it is Jesus Christ who is the distinctively Christian revelation? Our doctrines are but meditations on the revelation.

One more point and I shall have done with these preliminary observations. I start from an illustration. The author of Ps. 23 in a moment of high inspiration wrote, "The Lord is my shepherd." God so revealed himself to the poet that he could express what he saw only by calling him his shepherd. The image is found elsewhere in the Old Testament, but it does not seem to be common in early literature outside the Bible, though it is said to have been a Pythagorean doctrine that God is shepherd of the world, and I find that *poimen* or "shepherd" was at one time a cult name of Eros, the god of love. This will suffice for my present purpose. "The King of love my Shepherd is," as the hymn has it—are we to say that God revealed himself to the psalmist as shepherd, but that when the pagan spoke of the god of love as shepherd, it was no true inspiration but just a guess or a wish or a psychological projection? We should do better to suppose that the same God, the only God, put it into the heart of both Hebrew and pagan to declare, "The God of love my Shepherd is." But this would not imply an identity of

33

the revelation in the two cases. We must ask what is connoted for each by this term "shepherd." The insight of two poets using the same term may vary greatly in depth and penetration. Moreover, it is utterly impossible for us to define precisely what the Hebrew poet meant when he called the Lord his Shepherd. We can only surmise and argue from the metaphor. Yet these words of the psalmist have awakened in many hearts a response; through them God has made himself known as the Shepherd in many lands. The revelation is everywhere the same, yet different everywhere. Can "shepherd" mean the same thing to a Hebrew centuries before Christ and to a dweller in a modern city suburb? Can "shepherd" mean anything at all to the Eskimos? Moreover, to us the words of Ps. 23 convey meanings, cover connotations, carry overtones which could not possibly have been in the heart of the Hebrew writer; for it is Christ, the Good Shepherd, who interprets the words of the psalmist to a Christian; it is Christ whose presence may be conveyed to us through the psalmist's words. Because God is ever the same, the revelation is the same, for it is the one and only God who is revealed. But because men and ages are different, because insight varies enormously between man and man, the revelation is never twice the same. The revelation to me is not identical with the revelation to you, though we may use the same terms to express what we have seen. Yet the terms we use in common point to a truth which in some degree each of us has seen. I am stressing an obvious point, because I want to indicate how confusing and really unintelligible is the question often put by the ecclesiastically minded, "Do you accept the Christian revelation?"

"Shepherd" is not a theological term. It is obviously an image or a symbol. I put it to you that the great dogmas of the Christian Church are likewise symbols. The elabo-

34

ration of these symbols into theological formulas is a duty of the Church in each generation that it may, so far as possible, make its own faith intelligible to itself and others. But whereas the theological formulas are always changing, or ought always to be changing, the old symbols for the most part remain unchanged. I conclude with a quotation from John Oman,[3] whom, perhaps next to Plato, I regard as my greatest teacher. Oman speaks of the four veils that hide from our eyes the meaning of life's mystery, the veils of ignorance and sin, of weakness and evanescence. "Enshrouded by these four veils," he writes, "man stands before the mystery of God. By four great Christian doctrines they are taken away. The veil of our ignorance is removed by the Incarnation, the veil of our sin by the Atonement, the veil of our weakness by Grace, the veil of our evanescence by Immortality." These great truths, these great symbols, then, constitute the gospel. But let us remember that they are symbols, not definitions. As soon as we regard these great doctrines as metaphysical dogmas, says Oman, "we enter upon the most debatable of all human inquiries."

Before I come to what may be deemed the more constructive part of this book, I may conveniently sum up what I have ventured to suggest so far. First of all, I sought to reassure the more nervous and orthodox that I have no startling heresy of my own to dangle before your eyes, and to reassure the more venturesome and questioning and puzzled that I cannot feel myself bound by the letter of traditional theologies. I suggested that amid the theologies and confessions of the past we stand, as it were, in an impressive picture gallery, wherein all the artists from all the ages have sought to depict one

[3] *Vision and Authority* (London: Hodder & Stoughton, 1902), pp. 223-24.

face. We must allow all these portrayals to make their own impression on us, certainly not assuming that one is correct and all the others incorrect, but testing all by the portrait in the Gospels as we are able to recover it.

I then asked from what point we should start our theologizing. We cannot start without some presuppositions. We cannot theologize at all apart from the presupposition that God is, and that something may be known, is known, of him. I suggested that we should not close our ears to what God may be saying to us through any medium, whether nature or art, the Bible or the poets, the pagan philosophers or the Christian theologians. I then indicated that religious authority, that is, truly religious authority, is never dictatorial; it appeals to insight. It cannot be religious to accept alleged religious revelations if we can see neither rhyme nor reason in them, if they are not congruous with common knowledge, and if they do not awaken in us some awareness of God and evoke some religious response from us. I next asked what we are to understand by revelation. I urged that though we may not improperly speak about religious truths, propositions are not revealed ready-made from heaven. It is God who reveals, and it is God who is revealed. The propositions come later when we try to think out the implications of that which we have glimpsed. We must seek to express the self-revelation of God in words, but words are not the only media. I then urged that religious truths are "existential," so to call them; that is to say, they are addressed to the whole man, not merely to the intellect; they demand of us a response beyond our mere assent. I then urged that the truths of religion cannot be scientific truths; they are more like the truths of poetry; they are expressed in symbolic form. When we speak, as religious men must, of the acts of God, our language must be mythological and analogical. The language of religion, meta-

36

phorical, analogical, symbolical, points to the truth which we seem to apprehend; it cannot define or contain that truth; and whereas in the case of a scientific truth we either understand it or do not understand it, in respect of a religious assertion, such as "God sent his Son," we mean it, we believe it to be true, but at best we only begin to understand it.

2
Creation and Providence

Just as the denominational divisions which perplex and exacerbate Christianity in the West have little or no meaning for the younger churches of the East, so the old theological controversies of the past are often remote from the interest of the present generation. I dare not suggest that these old controversies were much ado about nothing, but to us they sometimes seem like a discussion whether we should print German in Roman or Gothic type, when we had not decided to use German at all. The Church has been divided, and is still divided, over such questions as whether the Holy Ghost proceeds from the Father and the Son or from the Father through the Son, whether the coming of Christ into the world was or was not attended by a physiological wonder, whether when God calls a man to the ministry, he minds very much who lays hands upon him in the act of ordination, whether God wishes us to be baptized as children or in later years. Very interesting points are these, no doubt, if you are sure that God exists and think that they matter very much; but they seem of an extreme irrelevance to many a man of the modern world; they do not deal with his intellectual perplexities at all; to him they are an obstacle to faith.

38

Our modern doubts lie further back; our burning questions are quite other. The controversies of the past are concerned with the principles or even the details of the redemptive dispensation, whereas our uncertainties gather about the very categories of human thought, space, time, causality, and substance, about the very existence of God and what, if anything, may be known and surmised about him. Moreover, there has been so great a revolution in human awareness that old questions, even where they seem relevant to us, present themselves in a new perspective, a new setting. The earth seemed very large and important when the sun and the stars were supposed to revolve around it; and even when it was at last accepted that the earth moves around the sun, men had no conception of the vast and unimaginable distances of time and space which modern astrophysics would reveal. The psalmist's question, "What is man, that thou art mindful of him?" takes on a new solemnity, even a new improbability, in the light of modern astronomical discovery. To this day much Christian thought remains still pre-Copernican. Was the universe really made for man, for his use and enjoyment, as Christians so often assert? Is man the last and ultimate word in creation? What can we surmise of other habitable worlds? What becomes of the once-for-allness, the *Einmaligkeit*, of the Christian revelation? Do B.C. and A.D. really point to a decisive turning point in the secular history of the galaxies? How insupportable is the thought of the power and majesty of God when we seek to imagine the vast universes revealed by mathematical calculation, the inconceivable smallnesses beyond the reach of the microscope! Is it sense to speak of the love of God for individual men or even for mankind as a whole? How could any sane man say of him now, "He loved me and gave himself for me"?

And as if these vertiginous riddles were not enough to overthrow all Christian faith, modern science has set new difficulties in our way. If, as I suppose, there is no necessary and ultimate quarrel between science and religion, since the existence of God is not a scientific question, yet there is, or there often seems to be, a great divergence between the world as science depicts it and the world as Christians have imagined it. The issue I may put in this way: both the natural scientists and the historians describe the world without finding it necessary at any point to bring in the name or the hypothesis of God. Neither party is under any intellectual obligation to deny that God or the Supreme Mind or the Great Mathematician may exist, but so far as this world in its progress is concerned, God seems to be irrelevant; nowhere can scientist or historian find him interfering in the causal order. God may be relevant to a world of fancy, sentiment, ideals, and mystical experiences, but to the world of science and history God's putative existence makes no practical difference at all. Let those pursue religion who have a penchant for that kind of thing, but in the practical affairs of life, in the study of science or history, God may be ignored. That vast engines should fly across the Atlantic would have seemed to earlier generations only possible by miracle. When I was young, satisfactory proof seemed available that such things in the natural order could not be; but they are, and there is nothing miraculous about them. The sphere of the miraculous, of divine interference, has grown less and less, till for the modern man there is no place for it at all. What is the good of praying for rain? Will God deflect bullets in response to our petitions? When we pray, does anybody hear? It is with issues of this ultimate and fundamental kind that we must deal, if we would relate religion to the burning issues of our time. Old controversies, as we might say, were about redemption; our problems lie further back; they concern creation itself and Providence. To these therefore I turn first.

I am not so foolish as to suppose that in a few paragraphs I can lay these ghosts that haunt the religious mind. I can but offer for discussion a few considerations, and first and perhaps most important of all is the consideration that one event may have several causes. There is nothing novel about this idea, but often it is forgotten, perhaps because scientists and historians in the course of their duty explain to us how A caused B, as indeed it did, leaving us to suppose that in this they have given not only an accurate but a full and sufficient account of the causation of the event under discussion. For the exposition of the present point I will borrow an illustration which, if my memory serves, is offered by Thomas Aquinas, but I will venture to elaborate it a little.

Let us imagine that on the grounds of "The Hermitage," near Nashville, a few generations ago there was stacked a cord of wood cut neatly into logs. The logs did not get there by accident; they did not put themselves there. What was the cause of their being there? You see at once that there are two possible answers: one, the scientific, in terms of haulage; the other historical, in terms of human activity. But let us analyze the situation in more detail. In order to make a tree into logs you must have a saw. It is a saw that makes logs. The saw, then, was the cause of the logs under discussion. But, as we know, a saw does not make logs of its own initiative; the hand and purpose of a sawyer are required. And while it seems accurate to say that the saw causes the logs, it is more adequate to say that the sawyer causes them. But, after all, the sawyer acted upon instructions; the tree was not his; he had no particular desire to saw logs; he would much rather have been idle in his cabin.

41

The real cause of the logs, then, was General Jackson himself, who instructed the sawyer to cut down the tree and saw it up. And why did General Jackson act as he did? I suppose because he regarded it as his duty to society, to his dependents, and to God that he should take care of his plantation, keep his buildings warm in winter and exercise the responsibilities of his calling. He acted in the way of duty. Thus the cause of the logs, in the end, was General Jackson's sense of duty, his duty to society, to his dependents, and so to God.

Should we not say then that in the last resort the cause of those logs is God? Or we might come to the same conclusion by another route. There could be no logs had there not been first a tree. Then we may ask what caused the tree. And if we pursued that elusive question far enough, I suppose that we should get back in the end through the long story of evolution to creation itself and so to God again. It would seem therefore that we might accurately assert that the tree caused the logs, that the saw caused them, that the sawyer caused them, that General Jackson caused them, that they were caused in the end by God. Each of these statements would be accurate; none of them by itself would be complete. The point of this long-drawn illustration is to remind you that in ordinary life we are familiar with the notion that one event may have several causes, each of which is a true cause in its own sphere. It would not occur to us to suggest that the explanation of the pile of logs offered by the scientist is incompatible with the explanation of the historian; and if religious men should wish to bring the name of God into the argument, this would not involve any questioning of what scientist or historian might have said.

The logs, as I have said, were not put there by chance; they did not put themselves there; they would never

42

have been neatly piled up there in what we are wont to call the ordinary course of nature: that is to say, they would not have been there but for man's intervention. But no one would suggest that there was anything miraculous about man's intervention; nature is responsive to the human will which intervenes in what we call the natural order and achieves ends which nature by herself, as we say, never could have achieved. I am not altogether happy about this way of putting the case; for in these days when modern man in his Titanism supposes that nature is there for him to tame, to exploit, to use as he in his folly may think best, it seems to me most important to insist that man himself is part of nature, one element in the created world. None the less it is convenient to speak of the exercise of the human will as altering the natural order. We are, in truth, very familiar with the fact that the spiritual or mental or nonmaterial can and does intervene in and alter the material and physical. A blush will rise to the face of beauty at a pretty compliment or, it may be, at an ill-timed story. Here the mental or spiritual directly affects the physical, but no one would call this miracle; it occurs in the natural order. But there seems to me an important corollary to this. If man by the exercise of his will, or as the direct result of his thought, can change and alter the processes of nature, producing that which otherwise would not have occurred, yet no one would suggest that herein there has been any breach of the order of nature or that the ordinary laws of cause and effect have been broken, I see no philosophical difficulty in the way of supposing that God, who holds the order of nature in being, may directly intervene in that order without any harm being done to the normal and unalterable laws of nature, which are of his appointment. If in the case of the logs we should say that God put it into the heart of General Jackson to

43

apprehend his duty in having the logs sawed and stacked in good time for the winter, we should have a clear case where God (on our supposition) intervened in the ordinary course of nature without any question of miracle in the sense of the suspension of natural laws. But could God, does God, intervene apart from human agency?

I think that scientists and historians from their point of view as scientists and historians are bound to maintain that every event in nature has its sufficient cause, that nature is in that sense a system of law, and that God, if indeed there be a God, does not "intervene" to set aside or break the laws of nature. I believe that William Temple once said of himself that his ignorance of science was so great as to be positively distinguished. I at least could make that claim with confidence on my own behalf. Perhaps for a Christian apologist to have no science at all is less dangerous than to have a little science. When some leading scientists recently declared that, as I understand, there is some unpredictable element in the behavior of electrons, many Christians were rashly disposed to think their cause much helped by this admission. The trouble with the scientists, however, is that they will not stop learning; what is scientific or orthodoxy one day may be an outmoded superstition before a few months are past, and it will not do for Christian theology or philosophy to be tied to some scientific theory which may prove transient. But I doubt whether any serious philosophical scientist still maintains the view that the universe is a mechanical system such that every event is mechanically determined by previous events. I am at least sure that the modern biologists and physicists do not hold that. But I think it entirely unsatisfactory that Christian apologists should excitedly claim that this just makes room for God to "intervene." I should much rather maintain that God never "intervenes."

44

When we look back, we can, if we are clever, always see how A was the cause of B. This applies both to history and to the natural sciences. When scientists would explain to us why this old oak tree is in precisely this condition and this shape, they must talk of wind and weather, of soil, of the action of men, or, it may be, of animals. They will not speak of the action of God. When historians explain to us the escape of the British from Dunkerque, which Sir Winston Churchill once called "a miracle," they will, if their information be sufficient, explain how the wind fell and the sea was calm for the small boats, how this shell falling here or there, So-and-So just escaped, how this road or that, being blocked by a fallen tree, was impassable at a critical moment for the German wagons, how General Kannsein, suffering slightly from intemperance, saw things a little askew through his glasses, and so on. They will not as historians speak of God; they certainly will not speak of "miracle." But no scientist who had watched the planting of the acorn from which that old tree grew could have predicted how the tree would grow, if indeed it should not be uprooted before it began to grow. No military historian would maintain that had he known the exact situation when the retreat to Dunkerque began, he could have predicted with certainty how many men would get away. The story of the universe may be described as the coincidence of law and contingency.

Am I laboring an obvious point? The natural sciences are in this sense abstract, so that the botanist may say, "If I can grow this acorn under laboratory conditions, if I can select the soil, control the temperature and the moisture, keep away children, pigs and pests, and eliminate all other contingencies, then I know that the acorn will grow in time into a tall oak, that is, if I live long enough to look after it." But he never would dream of saying

45

about any particular acorn in nature more than that if these conditions be fulfilled, and those be fulfilled, and nothing untoward should intervene, then the acorn will become an oak. It is not a question of miracles but of laws and contingencies. The military strategist may be confident that if the weather should hold, and if the air force should hit the targets, and if the enemy should do what he may be reasonably expected to do, then victory is certain. But every general knows how many unforeseen and unforeseeable contingencies arise. When we look back to past events, we can see how inevitably A caused B; when we look to the future, we can say little more than that A will cause B unless something should prevent it. By law we mean the dependable element in the universe, by contingency the unpredictable. It is not difficult to connect the idea of God with law, for we may say that the laws of the universe are the laws he has imposed upon it. But how shall we conceive the relation of God to the contingent?

Shall we claim that the contingent is the sphere of God's intervention? It may be that we make the issue unnecessarily difficult by this word "intervention." If you are driving an automobile, and suddenly a man or animal comes off the sidewalk just in front of you, I suppose that automatically your foot goes to the brake. You might, of course, quite accurately say that you "intervene" to prevent an accident by putting your foot to the brake, but that is not a word you would naturally use in such a context; the pressing of the brake is but part of your normal driving of the car. Because for very good and sufficient reasons science and history account for events without mentioning the name of God, we have an almost ineradicable notion that the universe is here and God is there, and he can come into contact with it only by poking his finger into it, as it

46

were, from the outside. But what if the driver and the car should be a more appropriate image? Even if it were, it is still a far from satisfactory image.

Let me come at the issue from another angle. I have spoken, as one does, of the existence of God and of modern doubts whether God exists. But the term "exists" is ambiguous in this context. Let me repeat the startling assertion of one of the greatest living theologian-philosophers, Paul Tillich, that God does not exist. God cannot exist, because he is the Ground of all existence. This is how Tillich puts it in his *Systematic Theology:* "However it is defined, the 'existence of God' contradicts the idea of a creative ground of essence and existence. The ground of being cannot be found within the totality of beings. . . . God does not exist. He is being—itself beyond essence and existence. Therefore to argue that God exists is to deny him." We cannot prove the existence of God, says Tillich: "The question of God is possible because an awareness of God is present in the question of God. This awareness precedes the question. It is not the result of the argument but its presupposition." This is not an atmosphere in which I can breathe for long, and I will not turn aside to discuss with you how near this is to the famous ontological argument of Anselm. Let me put the matter in simpler terms: we must not think of the universe as consisting of God and all the rest of the things that are. The universe is the totality of all things that are, and they are because God is their ground; they exist in him. God is not part of the universe but its presupposition and its ground. Just as we could have no idea of the physical world unless we were aware of it, so we could not have even the idea of God unless in some way we were aware of him.

Perhaps I have made a mistake in trying a shot out of Tillich's gun, when an arrow from the quiver of

Thomas Aquinas would have served me just as well. I certainly must not be understood as taking over the whole philosophy of Tillich. There is an extreme inadequacy in human words when we try to speak of God. Indeed there seems to me an element of utter impropriety, almost of blasphemy, in speaking about God. I have much sympathy with him who said that we should never speak about God; we should only speak to him. I have wanted to convey to you something of the mystery of God's being. We are so apt to think that God and the worlds make up the universe. That is why men think of miracle as one part of the universe, God, interfering with another part by intervention. God is not a part of the universe. It is convenient to say that the universe contains all things that exist. They exist because God created them and holds them continually in being. This means not that God does not exist, but that he does not exist in the same mode of existence as created things. After all, the idea that things can exist in different modes is not unfamiliar to us. We may say that the centaur, the mythical creature, half man, half horse, does not exist, never has existed, and could not exist. But a centaur does exist in another mode: it exists in our minds, and it is depicted in picture books. But the mode in which a centaur exists is a different kind of existence from that of actual men and horses. God does not exist in the same sense in which we exist but *sensu eminentiore*, as the Schoolmen say, in some more eminent sense. I am expounding not some agnostic naturalism with which I have no sympathy, but, at least in intention, the traditional doctrine of *analogia entis;* that is to say, there is an analogy between the being of God and our being or existence. We must never speak of God, in whom and through whom and unto whom are all things, as if he were one of the existences in the world about

48

whom we can speak as we can speak of all other things. But *patrii sermonis egestas*, indeed the utter inadequacy of all human speech is too much for me. We must therefore abandon this primitive picture of the universe as consisting of God and the rest of things that are, God being outside the world and therefore able to affect it only by poking it from time to time. The objections made by scientist and historian against the traditional idea of divine "interventions" are fully justified. God does not exist as if reality consisted of God and things. Rather, all things exist in God. God does not interfere with the natural order, for the natural order exists only in God. It is not for the scientist and historian as such to treat of God, but unhappy the scientist or historian who is not aware of God.

What, then, shall we suppose to be the relationship to God of the world of things with which science deals and the world of men which is the sphere of the historian? The theologian answers with his doctrines of Creation and of Providence. It is a traditional doctrine of the Church, resting upon Scripture, that God created the universe *ex nihilo*. It is extremely interesting that at the moment there is a tendency among scientists to regard creation out of nothing as a necessary postulate to explain the facts which they explore. Creation is a word that we use, but do not let us suppose that we understand it. It is a symbol pointing to that which exceeds our intellectual grasp. We cannot create; we can only make, or perhaps grow, from that which already pre-exists. There is some justification for the modern objections to the doctrine of creation. We cannot conceive a process of making something out of nothing; indeed, it could not be a process at all. We cannot conceive of a beginning of time, for we can always ask, "What happened ten minutes before that?" We cannot conceive of

49

an end to space, because we can always ask with Lucretius, "Where would a spear go if it were thrown from the outer edge of space?" But these natural objections to the doctrine of Creation rest upon a misunderstanding. There are, as the philosophers say, certain categories in terms of which alone we can apprehend the world, such categories as time and space, causality and substance; these afford the modes of our knowledge. When we assert Creation we do not mean that we are to think of God as somewhere and somehow making time and space and cause and substance; for the word "making" has no real meaning in such a context. What we assert is that God is the ground of the universe of all things that exist, that they exist in him in whom "we live, and move, and have our being."

But the Bible has more to say about nature than that in the beginning God was its creator. It will not allow that when the world had been created, God left it to itself. There is a doctrine of Providence also. We read that the Spirit brooded over the abyss and brought order out of chaos. The psalmists and prophets of Israel saw God's hand in all the events of nature and the happenings of history. The Lord God sent a strong east wind; the Lord rained fire and brimstone upon Sodom and Gomorrah; the Lord God destroyed Sisera and all his host. At a more philosophical stage Hebrew writers could speak of the Word or Wisdom of God sweetly ordering all things, and operative alike in nature and in the hearts of men. God clothes the lilies, feeds the ravens, numbers the very hairs of our head, and sends his rain upon the just and the unjust alike. Is such a conception of Providence intelligible and credible in the light of modern scientific knowledge?

Here I can offer three brief comments. The first is to remind you that we do not know, and cannot know,

50

Your Help Please!

Did this book meet your expectations? If so, why?
If not, please criticize.

ULTIMATE QUESTIONS

Please tell us what advertisement, review, or display influenced you to buy this book and from what source you bought it.

NAME————————————————
Your address is unnecessary; buy from your own bookseller!

WE PAY POSTAGE. SIMPLY FILL OUT AND MAIL WITHOUT STAMP

ABINGDON PRESS 150 Fifth Ave.
New York 11, N. Y.

in what relationship the created order stands to him who is its First Cause and its Ground. That is not a scientific question, nor is it a question that a created being ever could answer; we should have to be God himself to answer that. Second, I would remind you of my earlier argument that a single event may have many causes, each of which is a true cause in its own sphere, and I wish I had time and opportunity to expound to you the massive argument of Thomas Aquinas upon Providence and the virtual presence of God in all events. God is in everything that happens, as everything that happens is in God. In this connection I especially commend to your thought a notable saying of Nathan Söderblom, to the effect that a miracle is not an event that we do not understand; it is an event that we do understand, for no event is really understood until we see the hand of God in it. God does not "intervene" to break the natural order, which is his order, but he always uses it. Third, I would remind you how I indicated by the humble but familiar illustration of a blush that to our common knowledge the mental or spiritual, a sense of pride or a sense of shame, can directly affect the physical or material order without any breach in that order, and indeed as part of it. This we may properly call a scientific fact, a fact of common observation too. But if this is so, there is at least nothing irrational or unnatural or even strange in the belief that the physical order of the universe may be open, according to the structure of its nature, to the influence and movement of him in whom it has its being. God never "intervenes" in nature, because nature is always subject to his Providence.

I have been speaking of Creation and Providence, of the relationship of the created universe to him who is its Ground and in whom it has existence. I have urged that we are here in the presence of impenetrable mystery.

There can be no question here of proof; there can be no question of any symbol that shall in any degree be adequate. Yet some image we require for our thought and life, though we know it can be but an image. I have urged that it is wholly improper to speak of God's "interventions" as if he were part of the universe, a different part from the world with which he could come into contact only by action from without. Everything that exists exists in him. I suggested, but quickly dropped the suggestion, that the driver of a car would be a better image—better, perhaps, but utterly unsatisfactory. We know that there is a most intimate connection between our soul or our mind and the body which is its home and instrument, but the relationship between soul and body is an utter mystery. It has been suggested that the relationship between God and his created world is like that between soul and body. It is a nobler image, but we cannot very hopefully seek to interpret one mystery by another. We do not know, we cannot know, how the created world, and we as part of it, are related to him who made us or is making us. The image which seems to me most adequate is that of the relationship of an unborn child to the mother in whose womb it lives.

We cannot tell whether living creatures in the universe apart from man may be according to their mode and in some dim way aware of God. But it would seem that there is given to man a priestly function to perform in nature. The birds, the butterflies, the flowers praise God by being what they are, but do they offer conscious praise to him? It might seem to be the strange and wonderful prerogative of man alone among created things to offer conscious praise to God on behalf of all. You may regard this as fanciful, but at least it would seem plain that the relationship of rational and self-conscious beings to their Creator must be different from that of the inorganic and not yet self-conscious world. Let us then consider for a moment the relationship of rational man to God. I spoke previously of the various categories under which our experience comes to us, the categories of time and space, of causality and substance. There is one further category I must mention now, the category of the sacred. I shall expound that very briefly.

I suppose that a man who had no reverence for anything or anyone could scarcely be reckoned human. I define the sacred as that which is deemed to be of infinite worth, or to demand an unqualified obligation. That which is sacred is more important than life. To the man of science truth is sacred; he may never compromise with truth; to the artist beauty is sacred; he may never prostitute his art; to the Communist, atheist though he call himself, the obligation to serve what he conceives the coming age of universal felicity has claims upon him beyond his comfort or his life; things or fancied obligations which seem to us worthless and merely silly may be sacred to the savage, his fetish, his taboos, but they are of infinite worth or boundless obligation in his eyes; the claims of goodness, of loyalty, of country and home to us are sacred. There is no agreement among men as to what is sacred, but by the sense of the sacred, few if any are not touched. It is an a priori category. Just as a child may think that the lightning causes the thunder, and may thus misapply the category of causation, so a savage may deem that sacred which in fact has no intrinsic sacredness about it. But nothing is more mysterious about man, nothing more peculiar to him, than his reverence, whatever may evoke it. Now that which is of infinite worth, that which imposes an absolute obligation, that which is more precious than life itself, is something that transcends this mortal, transitory life where all is relative. We are in the sphere of the absolute, of the

53

infinite, of the eternal. It is in this sphere that dimly or consciously man is aware of God. There is a spiritual world impinging all the time upon this natural or physical world, and it is saints and poets and seers who most are conscious of this spiritual world through the category of the sacred. "Thy voice is round me like a bursting sea."

Here Tillich fruitfully distinguishes between what he calls "technical" reason and "ecstatic" reason. Our finite minds are normally confined to finite things; but every now and then, in a kind of ecstasy of the mind, we are aware of the mystery of the infinite and the eternal. But it is always, or nearly always, through the finite that we apprehend the infinite. From our point of view it is as if God makes himself known to us and deals with us in two diverse modes. With our natural technical reason we apprehend a world of law and order, a universe, the sphere of nature. This is the world with which both scientist and historian must deal. But every now and then through some particular event man (the scientist and historian as much as any other man) is aware of the underlying mystery, is aware of God, is touched with the infinite and the eternal, hears "far amid the fields of morn the rush of hidden wings," and this not in any contradiction of his technical reason but by a kind of ecstasy of reason. This is revelation. Since every finite event is related to the infinite (for the finite both pre-supposes and contradicts the infinite), since all things that exist exist in God, this strange rapture of the ecstatic reason may be evoked by any event whatsoever. This might be illustrated by the ancient legend of the Flood. We know, or the scientific among us know, what is the cause of the rainbow in the sky. The rainbow that appeared after the Flood came, we are told, to Noah as a revelation. It was to him a sign, a symbol, a promise,

54

an assurance of God's unfailing mercies, who never again would so overwhelm the world. To Brother Lawrence, as we read, the sight of a bare tree in winter was the occasion of his conversion; to another man

> a sunset-touch,
> A fancy from a flower-bell, some one's death,
> A chorus-ending from Euripides—
> And that's enough for fifty hopes and fears.[1]

Every event has its scientific aspect and its mathematical aspect and its historical aspect; and every event has, or may have, its religious aspect as it becomes the medium of man's awareness of the mystery of God. Tillich points out in a footnote to his *Systematic Theology* that whenever Bach's *St. Matthew Passion* is performed, a great risk is inevitably taken. The risk is that the hearers will be so caught by the sheer intellectual pleasure of the composition that they will miss the infinite to which the music points. So it was with the parables of Jesus Christ. Some heard the story, and that was that. To others the story opened a window into the mysterious, the eternal, the divine. There is no event that may not be the occasion of a revelation because no event happens except in God; every event therefore points to God, as it exists in God. The poets, the mystics, the seers, the "holy and humble men of heart" in every religion are they who are most constantly or vividly aware of this impinging of the eternal upon the temporal, of the infinite upon the finite. Revelation is a far wider term and concept than is comprised in the phrase "the Christian revelation."

Why should Noah in the story have seen in the rainbow the pledge and promise of the everlasting mercies? We detect no natural connection between the rainbow and the promise. Why should the sight of that bare

---

[1] Robert Browning, "Bishop Blougram's Apology."

tree in winter, coupled with the thought that soon it would again be clothed with leaves, have been the occasion of the conversion of Brother Lawrence? Many men since the dawn of history have contemplated trees in winter without conversion. We are here in the midst of the mystery of the unpredictable and the contingent.

One further illustration. We will suppose that an innocent young man who has but recently left home falls among convivial companions and enjoys himself one evening to excess. He awakens the next morning with a headache, *kraipale*, as the Greeks would call it. The headache follows the excess in the natural order; we will not say it is "sent" by God or "inflicted" by God, as if it came by some special interposition from on high. It follows in the normal order of cause and effect which God has appointed for us that we may be able to organize our lives. What is the result of this affliction? The man may be resentful and morose and may turn for comfort and restoration to "a hair of the dog that bit him." Indeed, if I could be fully persuaded by the literature of the Total Abstinence Movement, I think I should assert categorically that he had taken the first step on the downward path and that he would end as a sodden dipsomaniac. That might, it is true, be his depressing story. But a very different issue of the headache is quite possible. The man might be overcome with such mortification and shame and self-reproach that never again in all his life would be approach the danger point. He might even through this troublesome experience turn to God in penitence and learn for the first time what is meant by grace. No scientist, no historian, no philosopher, no psychologist could predict with certainty what would be the issue of that headache. Let this illustrate my contention that from our point of view God seems to act upon us in two diverse modes, the one impersonal, the other personal. The headache comes in the natural order, the sphere of cause and effect, God's impersonal dealing with us through the order of his appointment in the created world. But if, as is entirely possible, the headache should be the occasion of the young man's conversion, it would be an instance of God's personal dealing with a man through the impersonal order which the technical reason studies.

Let me put the same point in more theological terms. Every event may be not merely natural but also sacramental. A sacrament I should define as an event in which the material not merely represents but actually conveys the spiritual. It is here, if anywhere, that the term "miracle" will be in place. This "miracle" occurs not infrequently in connection with a sermon. Consider what occurs. A created being, not very wise, not very good, and probably very tired, prepares his sermon in his study. When he delivers his sermon, his words are but a physical thing, for they are breath. The sound waves strike upon some hearer's ear, and by some strange, unpredictable, inexplicable concourse of the divine Spirit with the speaker's words, the hearer is aware that the living God is dealing with his soul. It is but the same "miracle" when in the Communion Service the bread and the wine convey to the believing heart that which they are called to represent. I take the instance of church sacraments, but the principle is of far wider application. The human eye, marvelously compacted and constructed, is but a physical instrument. The letters printed upon the pages of a book are but conventional signs, without any intrinsic meaning of their own. You sit in your study; you read Plato and Dante and Shakespeare and Cervantes, the poets and the prophets, and through the material and the physical you are in touch with the great spiritual tradition of humanity, with God himself. Such is the mystery of matter, and it may one day prove that the real meaning and purpose of the material universe is that it should be the medium of the spiritual and eternal. But that is too hazardous a flight of speculation.

Let me briefly summarize my recent argument. I indicated to you that the burning theological issues of today are quite different from those which perplexed and divided the Church in earlier ages. Our hesitations, our dubieties lie further back. Theologians of the old schools may still dispute about the traditional teaching concerning the internal economy of the Trinity, about the relations of the human and the divine in Christ and the nature of the divine self-emptying, about the mode or scope of the Atonement. We shall not accuse them of discussing trifles; but the modern man is not even sure that there is a God at all, and if there be, how he is related to nature and history. It is the doctrines of Creation and Providence that are near to the heart of our perplexities today.

Creation, though it is a word sometimes used by scientists as well as theologians, is a symbol for that which we cannot comprehend. By the terms Creation and Providence we mean that this universe has its origin and ground in God, that it exists in God. But how in the light of modern scientific and historical methods of research are we to conceive the relationship of God to the world of nature and history? I suggested to you first that the same event may have many causes, each of which is sufficient in its own mode, and that we do not exclude the activity of God from nature and history if we wholeheartedly accept the validity of the arguments from cause to effect with which science and history must deal. The universe is a rational order wherein the incidence of B is explained by the prior incidence of A.

But in the rational order we find contingency as well as law. If God is the ground or author of the element of law, may we look also for his operation in contingency? The relation of the whole process to God is indeed impenetrable mystery, but I suggested that if God should put it into the heart of a man to do this or that, God would in this way be directly operating in the field of history, and I pointed out further that, as we well know, the spiritual or mental or nonmaterial can immediately influence and change the state of the material in certain cases; therefore, if in ways that we cannot conceive, the world exists in God, there is at least nothing irrational in the supposition that the material universe is open to the guidance and providence of God. And I suggested with all due hesitation that the image of the relationship of God to the world which seems to me least inadequate is that of the mother to her unborn child. In respect of man I further pointed to the "sacred" as a category in terms of which experience comes to man, and urged that this indicates a relationship between man and the infinite or eternal. Finally, I suggested that from our point of view God deals with us in two diverse modes, the personal and the impersonal. He deals with us impersonally in that nature which we explore in the light of "technical" reason; he deals with us personally through nature as he is apprehended by "ecstatic" reason, which is the medium of revelation.

Why is the universe as it is?

We may not tell why God made Sirius
  Nor Aldebaran, nor to what far end
The transient order moves ambiguous.
  The arcane purposes the stars subtend
  Mortal intelligence too far transcend,

That we, before the awakening Day, should pry
Into the counsels of Eternity.[2]

Why is history what it has been? What is the meaning
of our individual lives, if indeed they have any meaning? These are mysteries which go out far beyond our
comprehension. "Brethren, now are we the sons of God,
and it doth not yet appear what we shall be." Nothing,
I think, more offends truly religious men who do not
go to church than the bland assumption of some church-
men that we know the answer to these questions. How
fundamentally irreligious are all "slick" answers to ultimate religious questions! True faith is a kind of learned
ignorance. We should consider, too, that a process can
be understood only in the light of that to which it leads.
How could we know why the stars were made till the
immeasurable process which is the story of the universe
has been told and its purpose, whatever it be, accomplished? The meaning must lie outside or beyond the
process. The purpose of history must lie beyond history,
and the meaning of our lives on earth, if they have a
meaning, must lie beyond life on earth.

Yet we are not, or we should not be, the prey of a
total agnosticism here; for the veil has grown thin sometimes, and the silence has been broken in the assurances
of revelation. Piecemeal, it may be, and imperfectly,
according to their surroundings and their background,
the saints and seers and poets have received intimations
of that which "eye hath not seen, nor ear heard." We
have no knowledge of God unless it be by revelation,
and revelation, as I said earlier, comes in the form of
vision, not of information. How did Socrates know that
it is better to suffer evil than to do it? He could not
have learned that from this world, from science or his-

[2] From my *A Gallimaufry.*

60

tory. It came to him; he saw it; he knew it; he believed it, though his loyalty cost him his life. And I think we know it too. Therefore I am sure that out of the dark cloud God has spoken. Revelation, I repeat, is a wider term and concept than "the Christian revelation." But it is high time that I came to the Christian revelation.

3
The Jesus of History

What then is the Christian revelation? There is a type of religion which might not improperly be called the religion of all educated men who are in any degree religious. It is not a dogmatic faith, but it is not for that reason unimpressive. These religious men do not doubt that there is a God, they believe in Goodness, they trust, in spite of all misdoubtings, that there is a Friend behind phenomena. This is no ignoble faith, but it is not the Christian religion, though it may be surmised that it sums up sufficiently the practical faith by which many Christians live. The Christian faith is that God has not only spoken to us out of the great mystery that surrounds us; he has also come to us "in great humility" in the person of his Son, the Saviour of the world.

> Du den wir suchen auf so finsteren Wegen,
> Mit forschenden Gedanken nicht erfassen,
> Du hast dein heilig Dunkel einst erlassen,
> Und tratest sichtbar deinem Volk entgegen.

("Thou whom we seek on our so darkling ways, whom all our searchings cannot apprehend, once thou didst break through thy mysterious darkness, and camest visible to meet thy people.") There are no doubt ten thousand different ways in which the Christian apprehension may be expressed, but at the heart of them all, if they are in the great tradition of the centuries and of the New Testament itself, lies the conviction that in Jesus Christ God himself entered into the stream of history, and that his coming is for the salvation of mankind. I do not think we should be in the least surprised that to many not irreligious men of the modern world, brought up in the scientific disciplines of the present day, such a contention appears to be mere myth, phantasy, and nonsense. Is it a possible faith for the modern world? Are there any sufficient grounds on which we should believe it?

We are dealing with the alleged Christian "revelation." It is not to be claimed that this faith is to be demonstrated by the technical reason as a matter of scientific or historical fact. There are indeed certain historical facts connected with this faith; these are open to such proof as history admits of. But will the facts bear the conclusion or interpretation which Christians place upon them? The facts may be certain and be accepted; yet there may be no revelation. It is written of some that "their eyes were holden that they should not know him"; to some he was the carpenter; to others the prophet out of Galilee; others said, "He is beside himself"; and Thomas said, "My Lord and my God." In the light of modern scientific and historical knowledge, what can we expect the modern man to say of him? I think there are three typical answers open to the modern man. He may say that the historical records are insufficient to enable us to come to any judgment about Jesus Christ; or he may say that Christ was mad, or he may accept in some form the tradition of the Christian faith. I shall suggest to you that the first two answers raise difficulties for

63

thought as great as those they seem to resolve, and that however unsatisfactory are the language and categories in which the traditional faith of the Church has been expressed, we may as reasonable men give our assent to the substance of that faith.

Before I come to the difficulties of the historical question I must not wholly neglect an issue which seems of great significance to many men today. Lessing put the case most clearly in his assertion that the eternal truths of religion cannot be proved by the contingent facts of history. Does history, we may ask, really matter for religion? Truth is true whoever says it. If it be true that God is love, it remains true, though we may come to doubt the historical existence of him who is alleged first to have stated it. Does the historicity of Jesus really matter for religion? This is much too large and deep a question for me to answer in a paragraph. Let this much be said, however. If it really be true that God is love, the fact remains, even if it should be proved that Jesus Christ never existed. Nor should we deny that a man may believe that God is love and may order his life by that faith without believing in the historicity of Jesus, without even having heard of him. But we live in a world where the love of God for all men is by no means obvious, and where a large part of our experience seems to deny the love of God. Is not the existence of so much evil in the world the stock argument against the love of God? It is, as a matter of fact through history, and not as a result of speculation, that men in the West have believed in the all-embracing love of God. I should not wish to deny as a possibility that doctrines of God as love may be found in some form outside Christianity altogether, though I doubt it; I think we find only faint adumbrations of such teaching; but it is certain that if in other religions it is taught that God is love, yet "love so amazing, so divine" as is asserted in the Christian gospel is not to be found elsewhere. There can be no doubt whatever that the Christian doctrine of God as love comes to us from history and is inseparable from the belief in the historic cross of Jesus Christ. Further, suppose that some philosopher in his study should by thinking attain to a doctrine that God is love, giving to love the outgoing, condescending, unbreakable, redeeming quality which is what Christians mean by the love of God, such a doctrine would break down unless it were corroborated in the history of Jesus Christ. For I shall put it to you that the cross of Christ is the supreme test case in history. If he, being the kind of person we know him to have been, the just and innocent, died in shame and agony, mocked by his enemies, deserted by his friends, and abandoned by God, then what sense is there in speaking of the love of God as any kind of gospel? The doctrine that God is love, to keep to our illustration, is a philosophical proposition which is true or false whoever said it, but when we put the Christian meaning into the term "love," there is no doubt that this doctrine arises from history and must be rejected if this history be proved false. Truth is true, no doubt, whoever says it, but any proposition in the field of religion that claims to give meaning and significance to life needs the corroboration of life itself; it must answer to the facts. There is no getting away from history.

But is historical research a science? Can events of the past be proved? Can we attain to more than probabilities, and can religion rest on probabilities? In particular, can the Gospels really be trusted?

It will be admitted by all serious scholars that there are many points of uncertainty and obscurity in the Gospels. But our modern doubts go beyond all details.

I well remember that many years ago I read through Mark's Gospel at a sitting, attempting, so far as possible, to read it with fresh eyes as if I had never read the story before and had picked it up by chance in a railway bookstore. I said to myself, when I came to the end, that if I were not a Christian, I should not believe a word of it. By this I meant that had I come to this narrative as a stranger, with the presuppositions with which one properly comes to the study of an alleged historical document, I should have been compelled mentally to reject and, if possible, explain away very much that I there read. Not merely should I feel that there were palpable legends interspersed in a narrative that might otherwise be historical, but, rather, the whole narrative is so suffused with the supernatural, both in its setting and content, as to leave no clear historical impression. I was no doubt at a skeptical age in a skeptical period, but on the presuppositions with which I attempted to approach the book, I fancy that my reaction was quite natural.

But there is another side to the question. I was very greatly impressed when I read *The Idea of Christ in the Gospels* by George Santayana. He approached the Gospels from another angle. He did not believe that there is any historical basis for them whatsoever. Never, therefore, in his exposition is he troubled by questions of historical probability or possibility. He has no sympathy with theological "liberals" who would dilute or rationalize or explain away awkward elements in the Gospel narratives. He takes all four of them together as they are, and he elaborates the picture of Christ which they have drawn for us. He recognizes, of course, that there are differences between them, but together they present a homogeneous portrait of the Christ. The figure whom he thus depicts is the Christ of the Church's faith.

For himself he believes that this person so depicted is quite unhistorical, and he asks us to believe that this marvelous picture of such a One as the world never dreamed of before was actually botched together by a committee, and, at that, a committee which never met!

Here, then, from the beginning we are presented with a dilemma by the Gospels: such a Person never could have lived; such a Person never could have been invented! Which horn will you choose? I shall revert to this dilemma. Let it suffice for the moment that we may not bid men lay aside, as they read the Gospels, their critical judgment and the natural dictates of their reason. We may urge, however, that if they come to the study of the Gospels seeking some clue to the mystery of life and death, they may, as they read, become aware of the abyss of mystery, of the eternal and the infinite, of God, in such a way that elements in the story which would else seem fabulous, may take on another hue, for we are sure that to the listening ear the Gospels speak an infinite and eternal word.

If the Gospels should be isolated from all the rest of literature and from all the history with which they are connected, if they should be treated as dead facts "stranded on the shores of the oblivious years," the impulse to explain them away as interesting relics of a romantic movement in religion would be almost overwhelming. But the Gospels do not stand alone or isolated. They are not intelligible alone. It may be well to start our historical inquiry not from the person of Christ as depicted in the Gospels, but from the Christian community out of which the Gospels spring. Here our feet seem to tread on surer ground.

We have considerable historical knowledge of affairs in the Mediterranean basin in the first century of our era. Christianity came into a chaotic, distracted, disillusioned world. The old religions had lost their hold except among the Jews. In Palestine and elsewhere the barrier between the Jews and the Gentiles, mere "dogs of the concision," showed the racial problem in its most intense form. It was a world of slavery, of astrology, of power politics, of nationalism, of hatred, and of selfishness. I would not paint too dark a picture of it. It was a world much like our own in its tensions and disillusionments. In the world of these dark shadows, these fears and tensions and superstitions, there suddenly appeared the Christian Church, which we know chiefly from the correspondence of Paul that has been preserved for us. I cannot go here into technical questions of literary criticism. It is entirely possible that all the so-called Pauline writings have been edited into the form in which we have them. In the instances of II Corinthians and the Pastorals this is certainly the case. It is quite possible, as a number of excellent scholars have supposed, that the apostle Paul is not the author of one or two of the letters ascribed to him by uniform tradition. But it will not be disputed that, at the very least, in Romans, I and II Corinthians, Galatians, and Philemon we have a very substantial body of the indubitably authentic writings of the Apostle to the Gentiles. Indeed, it will not be disputed, even by scholars who are much more hesitant about many passages than I am disposed to be, that from the pages of the New Testament we can draw a reliable, if partial, picture of these first communities of Christians. The apostle writes to groups composed of Jewish and Gentile converts who, whatever their weaknesses, which were great and many, offered to the world a quite new type of society, in which racial, social, and economic divisions had been overcome, in which the praise of the goodness of God and the love of the brethren were the distinguishing marks. His readers know as a matter of personal experience that they have been translated out of darkness into a world of marvelous light, that the dark oppressive demonic forces of fate or Satan or the evil spirits have been overcome. He exhorts them to love, to patience, to contentedness, to praise, "Rejoice, in the Lord always: and again I say, Rejoice." He reminds them that as a matter of their own experience they have received a Holy Spirit; they were, as it were, re-created or born again into a new world; they were a colony of heaven on earth.

How are we to account for the appearance of these new communities, their vitality, their spread, their emancipation from all the oppressive fears and superstitions and divisions of the age, their spiritual hilarity, that which a later poet calls "the sober intoxication of the Spirit" (*sobriam ebrietatem Spiritus*)? Nor does the story end with the Pauline epistles and the New Testament itself. The story of the Christian Church is no doubt a very mixed story, in many ways a very worldly story; it is perhaps the most heartbreaking fact in history. Yet it is on the other hand the most wonderful and the most heartening fact in history. The result of this Christian movement, so obscure in its first beginnings and so marred by human folly and sin throughout, has been so stupendous that universal history is properly divided into two parts, the years before Christ and the years of our Lord. There have been many bad Christians, but we all know what we mean by the phrase "a real Christian." It is the "real" Christians whom we might call the soul of the Church. The Church has never been without a soul! How are we as historians to account for these early communities of Christians to whom the New Testament points, how are we to account for "the soul of the Church" thereafter through the centuries, the characters it has produced, the achievements to be ascribed to it? What cause is adequate to this effect?

I must not at this point expatiate upon the experience of Christians. I have admitted that there is a deplorable side to church history, and I cannot think that my present argument will carry any weight with those who are indifferent to religion, or who by reason of their upbringing or their unfortunate experience with churches or Christians have been deeply alienated from the Christian faith. But it will carry some weight with those who view a "real Christian" with a sort of wistful reverence, who are feelingly aware of what the Bible and the Christian religion have meant in the history of this country, and who have some idea of the spread and influence of Christianity in Europe first, then in the Americas, then in Asia, then in Africa, and in the islands of the southern seas, and who more recently have had occasion to observe the Christian Church under the Nazi persecution and behind the Iron Curtain. I would plead, then, that if the story of Jesus in the Gospels, the picture of him there, is true or substantially true, then the experience of the early Church, the life, the achievements, the experience of Christians since those days, become intelligible and are accounted for. If, on the other hand, the story in the Gospels be rejected as fabulous, how are we to explain the sequel? Of course our inability to find a sufficient cause would of itself prove nothing. But a historian or serious person wants to understand, and if he cannot explain, he cannot understand. The story of the world since Christ has been very largely the story of the influence of Christ upon the world. Can it all rest upon the pious and baseless imagination of a group of writers who wrote for the most part independently of one another or upon the hallucinatory experiences of a

70

few obscure Jews who foolishly thought their Master had risen from the dead? I would not press my argument too far, but may urge that in reading the Gospels with an open mind and with intellectual integrity, we should come to them not merely with the presuppositions with which we approach any story from the past, but also with the consciousness that "Christianity" as a factor in world history must somehow be accounted for.

I would plead with the hesitant man of the modern world that he approach the Gospels with an open mind. I would plead with the dogmatists that they too would approach this study with an open mind. I do not mean that they should try to come to the study of the Gospels as if they were not men of faith, but for two reasons I would beg them not to come with preconceived and immovable theories of the nature of the person of Christ. The first reason is that although in principle the Church has always maintained from the beginning that Christ was very Man as well as very God, yet in fact his alleged humanity has been swallowed up in his divinity in traditional Christian thinking, Orthodox, Medieval, Protestant, and if we read the Gospels through the spectacles of inherited Christologies, we preclude ourselves from the serious study of historical documents. The second reason is that if we read on the assumption that he was the God-man, or God and Man in one, or both Son of God and Son of man, we shall think we understand, but do we know what our words mean? Can we imagine or conceive what a God-man would be? I am saying not that these doctrines are untrue but only that if taken literally and as explanations, the words are almost meaningless. The right procedure for Christians as for all others is *per Jesum ad Christum*, through Jesus as he is known in history to the Church's faith in him. Let Christians

71

bring to the study of the Gospels what faith and experience they may have. Let them come with an open and fearless mind; then, it may be, they will begin to understand these old doctrines as tremendous symbols intelligible to faith, perhaps even necessary to faith, but never by way of theory and explanation.

Jesus Christ is a historical personage. There is no doubt about that. I suppose that there is no historic fact beyond the scope of living memory which can be proved against an ultimate skepticism, but there are many facts which only a partial lunatic would doubt. No one in his sober senses doubts the Norman conquest of England, the American War of Independence, the historicity of Alexander or of Socrates or of Julius Caesar. That Jesus was a real person, that he lived and taught in Palestine, that he was crucified under Pontius Pilate in the first half of the first century of our era, is not in doubt. But what more do we know about him for certain? We may properly claim to know that he was raised within Judaism, that he lived within Judaism, that his mission was in the first instance to the Jews, that he worshiped with Jews as a Jew and though he quarreled with the religious leaders of his people and was rejected by them, he never broke with the religion of his ancestors. Perhaps I should have said first of all that he was a man, a real man. Here technical theologians will take me up and claim that he was man but not a man. I will therefore amend my statement and say that he seemed to be a man, that no one who saw him doubted that he was a man; he lived as a man; he died as a man; he prayed as a man. Upon that last point I will lay stress. We know that he prayed. It is said that he spent a whole night in prayer. The traditional theologians of the Church, John of Damascus, for instance, or Thomas Aquinas, have been very hard put to it to explain, or rather to explain away,

72

his prayers. If, as they said, he was very God, was he really praying to himself; were his prayers quite real? Never mind for the moment what happens to our theories; we may be quite sure that we are getting away from facts when we do not take very seriously and literally the evidence that he prayed. During his lifetime no one doubted that he was a real man.

What kind of man was he? Here I do not call your attention to the Gospels first, because with the possible or probable exception of the Fourth Gospel, we cannot safely ascribe the Gospels to eyewitnesses; the earliest of them was written probably after the death of Peter and Paul. But we have some evidence which, though mostly indirect, is indubitably contemporary evidence, namely, in the correspondence of the apostle Paul, who was the contemporary, though perhaps the younger contemporary, of Jesus. He may have seen Jesus, but on the whole it is generally thought that he did not. But he certainly knew those who had known Jesus. He knew James, the Lord's brother, as he himself tells us; moreover he describes in one of his letters how, as he puts it, he went up to Jerusalem "to learn Peter's story" (*historêsai Kephan*) and spent two weeks with him. Moreover, Paul had been pre-eminent as a persecutor of the new sect; he had passively participated in the lynching of Stephen. Paul the persecutor knew all that could be said against the Christian sect and its testimony to Jesus. He knew both sides of the controversy; he was the contemporary; we could not have a better witness.

Nowhere in his extant correspondence does Paul set out to describe the character of Jesus, but his letters are full of ethical teaching. This takes the form of exhorting his readers to "walk in the Spirit," to be guided by the Spirit, to live as those who are "in Christ." He tells them what manner of people they will be if they walk in the Spirit. This he does constantly, but perhaps pre-eminently in I Cor. 13, the famous passage where he says: "Charity suffereth long, and is kind; charity envieth not; charity vaunteth not itself, is not puffed up, doth not behave itself unseemly, seeketh not her own, is not easily provoked, thinketh no evil, rejoiceth not in iniquity, but rejoiceth in the truth; beareth all things, believeth all things, hopeth all things, endureth all things." Elsewhere he exhorts his hearers: "Let love be without dissimulation. . . . Be kindly affectioned one to another with brotherly love; in honor preferring one another. . . . Rejoicing in hope; patient in tribulation; continuing instant in prayer; distributing to the necessity of saints; given to hospitality. . . . Recompense no man evil for evil. . . . If thine enemy hunger, feed him; if he thirst, give him drink. . . . Be not overcome of evil, but overcome evil with good." How different from Confucius' ideal or Aristotle's or even Cicero's! That is the kind of person we shall be if we are guided by the Spirit. But whence did Paul and his contemporaries get this ideal, this vision of what human life might be and ought to be? There is only one possible answer: they got it from Jesus. Paul is quite explicit about it, for the Spirit of which he speaks is, as he tells us, the Spirit of Jesus: "Now the Lord is the Spirit." Thus in these passages and elsewhere Paul is describing what we shall be like if we are moved by the Spirit of Jesus. Indirectly he is describing Jesus. We cannot honorably set aside this contemporary evidence as to the kind of person Jesus was.

What, then, did Jesus do? I am asking a historical, not a theological, question. To use one of the simplest expressions of the Bible, he "went about doing good." He

74

healed the sick and cast out demons, or, as we might say, he cured the demented. A generation ago these "miracles of healing" were a stumbling block to the rationalism of the day, but now I suppose no one doubts that he healed the sick. We have, of course, no satisfactory medical diagnosis of his cures, but that he was as Paul describes him, that he went about doing good, and that he healed the sick cannot be doubted. When Pilate said, as is reported, that he found no evil in him, he was speaking less than the truth; for I have not yet mentioned one of the most remarkable or portentous things that he did, a new thing in the world: he sought out as the particular recipients of his compassion the "publicans and sinners," the people who because of their double life or neglect of religious duties were regarded by the upright as especially the subjects of divine displeasure. He never condoned their sin, but he went out of his way to be their friend. I may refer to a single story about him which is textually suspect, but as to the historical authenticity of which there will be no dispute. The scribes and Pharisees had brought to him in some public place a woman taken in adultery; it is well that we attempt by an act of historical imagination to visualize the scene. "They say unto him, Master, this woman was taken in adultery, in the very act. Now Moses in the law commanded us, that such should be stoned; but what sayest thou? This they said, tempting him, that they might have to accuse him." What will he say? In God's name what will he say? What gospel will there be for you or me or any man if he shall fling her back to them and loathe her? "But Jesus stooped down, and with his finger wrote on the ground, as though he heard them not. So when they continued asking him, he lifted up himself, and said unto them, He that is without sin among you, let him first

75

cast a stone at her. And again he stooped down, and wrote on the ground. And they which heard it, being convicted by their own conscience, went out one by one, beginning at the eldest, even unto the last: and Jesus was left alone, and the woman standing in the midst. When Jesus had lifted up himself, and saw none but the woman, he said unto her, Woman, where are those thine accusers? hath no man condemned thee? She said, No man, Lord. And Jesus said unto her, Neither do I condemn thee; go, and sin no more." That is what he was; that is what he did.

Let us consider what he said. It is here that our difficulties begin. What he was in his character and what he did are facts which may excite our wonder but in no way affront our reason; but with some of his sayings it is otherwise. Part of his teaching, no doubt, is parallel to that of Paul, in the passages we have considered; here his own life is the best commentary upon what he taught. But he was certainly not a professional or systematic ethical teacher; as little was he a systematic philosopher or theologian. His sayings are mostly brief, occasional, episodic; but his theme, as nearly all scholars would agree, was "the kingdom of God," which he declared to be "at hand." What does this phrase mean, and how is it to be translated into modern English?

It is a pleasing thought that I am now about to answer in a few paragraphs a question about which libraries have been written by the learned, and upon which there is at present no clear agreement. I think, however, that I can say a few simple things which would meet with very general agreement.

I may start from what we are wont to call the inaugural vision of the prophet Isaiah which came to him "in the year that King Uzziah died." There may well be some special connection between the king's death and

76

Isaiah's vision. For Uzziah, as tradition tells us, had lived through a long reign which, at least in its earlier stages, had seemed glorious. Moreover, in those early days he had been a religious man and had reigned as such. But it may well be that the sense of power "went to his head," as we say. So it has been with many men in positions of undisciplined authority. Uzziah, we are told, had claimed to be not only king but also priest, and he was smitten with leprosy and died a leper. The kingship had long been established in Israel, but the tradition had not died that the real king, the supreme king of all the earth was Jehovah, God. In the year that the earthly king died, so smitten and so dishonored, Isaiah saw the Lord, the King, upon his throne, and around him were the heavenly seraphim singing their song of praise and adoration which the prophet overheard. It came to him that they were singing, "Holy, holy, holy, is the Lord of hosts: the whole earth is full of his glory," words still very familiar in the Christian liturgy, "Heaven and earth are full of his glory." Were these words true or false? If they were true, their truth was, as concerned most men, an unsuspected secret. Reverting to the terminology of Tillich we may say that the prophet Isaiah, by an act of ecstatic reason, apprehends the ultimate Ground of all things, and realizes, in spite of all appearances to the contrary, that all things are a manifestation of God's glory.

> Earth's crammed with heaven,
> And every common bush afire with God;
> And only he who sees takes off his shoes—
> The rest sit round it and pluck blackberries.[1]

With this apprehension that the whole earth is full of

[1] Elizabeth Barrett Browning, *Aurora Leigh*, Bk. VII, 1. 820.

God's glory we may properly compare some of the sayings of Jesus Christ about the kingly rule of God. Every Jew and, for the matter of that, every pagan in Palestine was aware of the vagaries of the weather. But Jesus Christ in his profound consciousness of God apprehended in and through the weather the ultimate Ground of being and touched God: "Your Father . . . in heaven . . . sendeth rain on the just and on the unjust." His tender mercies are over all his works. Not a sparrow falls to the ground but the Father knows; behold the lilies of the field: they manifest God, they speak of God, they are the very works of God, they are the media of God's presence. Jesus was not thinking of what we call "the laws of nature," but certainly he was not denying them. The laws of nature are apprehended by the technical reason; God's presence in and through them is apprehended by the ecstatic reason. Part of what Jesus Christ meant when he summoned men to enter the kingdom is that he was calling them to recognize God's fatherly providence in and through all things, so that they need take no thought for food and drink and what the morrow might bring forth, living on "the sparrow and the lily principle," trusting their heavenly Father for all their needs, "The whole earth is full of his glory."

Such should life be according to what Renan once called "the Galilean idyl." But life is not idyllic, nor was the teaching of Christ when taken as a whole. We may conveniently revert to Isaiah's vision. Its immediate effect upon him seems to have been the awakening of a sense of guilt. "Woe is me!" he cried, "for I am undone; . . . for mine eyes have seen the King, the Lord of hosts." The prophet knows himself for a man of unclean lips who lives among a people of unclean lips. Granted that the whole earth is full of God's glory, yet this is hidden from mankind, from the people of unclean lips and unclean hearts. As Augustine Birrell once put it in his nontheological way, "There is a sore wound at the heart of humanity." Of this we too are very conscious. By Jews of later generations this sense that something had somehow gone wrong with creation was expressed in the view that this present age, the age in which all men live, is subject not to God, but to Satan, or is subject to God only in some such limited way as that for the moment it is the realm of Satan and the dark satanic powers. By a startling paradox, Jesus Christ, who saw the fatherly hand of God in all things, seems also in some way to have shared in this other view. In his work he saw "Satan as lightning fall from heaven"; he spoke of a poor woman "whom Satan hath bound, lo, these eighteen years." This is the language of myth, of picture. We cannot answer the question how far, if at all, Jesus and his contemporaries intended this conception of the realm of Satan literally or scientifically. Those are modern questions that reflect the modern outlook. It seems certain, however, that Jesus deemed it his mission to deliver men from the bondage of Satan; he was "the stronger" who casts out the strong man. "If I with the finger of God cast out devils, no doubt the kingdom of God is come upon you." In other words, he not merely called men to see the fatherly hand of God in nature and to trust him; he came also actively to deliver men from the tyranny of evil and bring them into a new world, the kingdom of God. This is exactly expressed by the apostle when he speaks of God as translating us out of darkness "into the kingdom of his dear Son."

I return once more to the Old Testament. It is the theory of one very distinguished Scandinavian scholar, Sigmund Mowinckel, that every New Year the Hebrews celebrated the festival of the Enthronement of Jehovah. This celebration gathered around the myth that the earthly king, the anointed representative of God, suffered appalling disaster, and that when all seemed lost, Jehovah stretched forth his right hand in a mighty and signal deliverance. This theory has not won universal acceptance. If true, it would throw remarkable light upon many of the psalms, and—a point upon which I should be disposed to lay much stress—it would afford some explanation of the fact, so strange to us, that the passion and resurrection of Christ are regarded in the New Testament as plainly adumbrated in the Scriptures. Thus Paul gives it as part of the accepted tradition of the Church that "Christ died for our sins according to the Scriptures" (what Scriptures can be meant?) and that "he rose again the third day according to the Scriptures" (what Scriptures can these be?). Even if Mowinckel's theory should not win acceptance, some such myth or intuition or symbol of disaster, followed by the great deliverance, may be deemed to lie behind the strange words of Jesus Christ, "It is necessary that the Son of man should die." Here as often elsewhere we cannot separate between what he said and what he did; he deliberately "set his face to go to Jerusalem"; he deliberately challenged his enemies in the very seat of their power; he went to his death with deliberation, "I, if I be lifted up from the earth, will draw all men unto me"; "this cup is the new covenant in my blood"; "I will not drink henceforth of this fruit of the vine, until that day when I drink it new with you in my father's kingdom." His suffering and death were necessary that the great victory might be won and the kingdom realized in the future beyond his death.

I have indicated to you three "moments" in the teaching of Jesus about the kingdom: first, the realization of God's fatherly rule and his actual kingship now; second, the present reign of Satan and man's deliverance from

80

the power of Satan now; third, the prediction of a future kingdom through his death and beyond history. It will, I think, generally be agreed among technical scholars that all these three elements are present in his teaching.

Such was his teaching. But was it true, or was it largely a delusion? Was it only paradoxical or merely incoherent? This is a question we cannot in honesty avoid. Jesus asserted God's fatherly love and providential care for all his children; he bade men trust God on the ground that he who cares for the sparrow will much more take care of them; he seems to have regarded ill health as one of the works of Satan. A pretty romance is what men will call this, and will point us to the fate of this romantic teacher; did not his own story give the lie to everything he taught? If ever there was a true son of God who trusted his heavenly Father and did his will, that man was Jesus. He at least was "the just man." It might perhaps be said of all others that they suffer for their sins, but that could not be said of him. Is God really to be trusted, or is this a God-forsaken world? This was the test case in all history. Jesus trusted utterly in God, and he died in agony, forsaken by his friends and apparently abandoned by God himself: "My God, my God, why hast thou forsaken me?" What other conclusion can men draw than that Jesus was the Deceiver of mankind, himself the great Deceived, and that this is a God-forsaken world?

The Jews of that day held that the present age is the reign of Satan, but that God in his own good time would intervene and bring in the new age, the kingdom and rule of God. The hearts of many were full of wild apocalyptic hopes that the new age would presently appear, and history, as we know it, would be ended. It is very difficult for us imaginatively to realize the excitement, the tension, the hopes that would be raised when, at the very beginning of his ministry, Jesus came into Galilee declaring that the time was fulfilled and the kingdom was at hand. In other words, the hour has struck, God is about to act decisively in human history. His words seemed at first to find corroboration in what happened. True, he disappointed nationalistic hopes by resolutely refusing to give a lead against the hated Romans; true, he quarreled with the religious leaders of the time in his rejection of their tradition; but he performed wonders of healing and spoke words of marvelous hope and comfort; these might be taken as the signs or even as the first fruits of God's decisive act. Yet in themselves they fell far short of the revolutionary and world-shattering announcement that the kingdom of God is at the door.

We may surmise that had his ministry been limited to "the Galilean idyl," many, including Coué, might have drawn important psychological lessons from it, but certainly it would have been no grappling with the powers of evil in the world. There was no decisive battle, no decisive victory. It would seem, indeed, that Jesus himself was, as it were, embarrassed by the success of his healing ministry; he bade men be silent about their cures. It was not primarily to such a ministry that he was called. It would seem more near the truth to say that he felt called to die. We note how at the end he like a magnet seemed to gather against him all the powers of evil in the world, the power politics of Rome represented by Pontius Pilate, the worldliness of the Herodians, the ecclesiasticism of the Pharisees, the indifference of the common people.

There was, so far as we can see, no historical need for him to die; he could have retired into obscurity; he might have written a book and sheltered himself behind a pseudonym. When near the end "the Greeks" wanted to see him, what an opportunity must have opened before his weary eyes! Why should he not go to Athens, where they were always glad to hear some new thing, to Alexandria, where a more liberal Judaism would be more responsive to him; he might, indeed, have become an itinerant preacher in the Roman Empire, like the Stoic evangelists of his time. He sent the Greeks a cryptic answer: "Except a corn of wheat fall into the ground and die, it abideth alone: but if it die, it bringeth forth much fruit." He could have escaped death quite honorably, so far as we can see, but, instead, he seemed to seek it. Yet his going up to Jersualem was not constructive suicide. It was his last appeal to his own people. Remember that not all those who rejected him were evil men; many were good men by our standards. The best was rejected not only by the worst but also by the second best. That was the tragedy! Could they defeat him, or would he defeat them? The shadow of the Cross lay athwart all his days, but we cannot know at what point he knew for certain that he would be killed, that his life by every outward standard would end in irreparable defeat for him and disaster for his friends and for his cause. What could he do alone, unarmed, against the might of Rome, with his enemies around him and with the support only of a little group of friends who could not understand him and at a pinch would all desert him? What tragedy, what folly that he, a young man, should die with no book written, no friend to support him, none to understand him, with everything he had

83

tried to teach and to do in jeopardy! But he, "the young prince of glory," by an almost inconceivable act of faith in God risked everything upon his confidence that through his death there would be a decisive act of God, that the kingdom was at hand. He sets us the inescapable question of faith, whether or not he was mistaken.

4
The Resurrection

Jesus declared that God is utterly to be trusted, that God was about to act decisively, that the kingdom was at hand; and so he died on the cross, forsaken, as it seemed, by God and man. Was he mad? Or did God vindicate his faith? That is the question of the Resurrection, and compared to it all minor details of the resurrection stories are of no importance. What, then, is meant by the Resurrection, and did Christ really rise again? Was this an event of which historians should take account? Can we of the modern scientific age with any confidence or with any understanding assert the Resurrection?

There are puzzles here that most certainly I cannot solve. Some clever people claim to derive a clear and consistent and consecutive picture from the various sources that come down to us, but this must be by some intellectual tour de force. Let me put some of the puzzles to you frankly. The apostle Paul, our earliest writer, perhaps our one contemporary writer, says that after his resurrection the Lord appeared to Peter first. That is not what the Gospels say. There is good reason for supposing that the appearance to Peter was the turning point in the recovery of the disciples' faith; but why is there no reference to it in Mark's Gospel, which is usually supposed to be peculiarly related to that apostle? There is apparently some account of it in the Fourth Gospel, but there it is located in Galilee, whereas in the other Gospels we find the holy sepulcher narratives instead. Paul also tells us that the Lord appeared to James, but concerning this the Gospels are altogether silent; he never mentions the appearances to the women or the empty tomb; he also refers to an appearance to some five hundred brethren, which mystifies us entirely, unless perhaps this is his account of Pentecost.

Then, again, when did the Resurrection happen? Was it "after three days and three nights," as indicated by the reference to Jonah in the belly of the whale? Or was it "on the third day," that is, on the Sunday morning after the Friday of the Crucifixion? This is the commonly accepted view; but if, as we read in one Gospel, the departed saints rose from their graves and walked in the city on the night of the Crucifixion, surely Christ must have risen too. This may seem an entirely legendary story, but it corresponds to the long-continuing practice of some (Quartodeciman) churches which on the same day celebrated both the Crucifixion and the Resurrection. Was the Resurrection an event that really could be dated?

Once more, granted that many disciples had, or thought they had, a vision of Christ after his death, what kind of vision was it? Were there hallucinatory elements in it? Did they behold a Christ of flesh and blood who could be touched and who could eat? If he did not rise, what happened to his body? Why did not the Jews produce it and strangle the new heresy at its birth? Did Christ rise with a "glorified" or "spiritual" body, and if so, what may that be? What of the scientific implications of it? And did he appear in garments that were likewise "glorified" or "spiritual"? We cannot with any confidence answer these questions, nor may we put them aside as wholly illegitimate.

I may be permitted to observe that the resurrection stories in the Gospels are in the technical sense to be ranked as "legends," that is to say, they are *legenda*, stories to be read for edification in the worship of the Christians. This does not of itself imply that any of them is untrue, but all that we can say with certainty about most of them is that they point to that stupendous fact or belief which was the basis of the Christian faith and of the Church's life. This fact—for I shall call it such—is in part historical, but it is also a spiritual or religious apprehension. That which we call the Resurrection points to a historic fact which within narrow limits can be dated, but it was no mere physical wonder. Did not Jesus himself say, "If they hear not Moses and the prophets, neither will they be persuaded, though one rose from the dead"? Suppose we could prove as a matter of history that his body disappeared "into thin air," as we say, or that it suffered some kind of sea change such as Spiritualists might be willing to explain, would that account for the Christian movement? Would the world be any better off for that assurance? Would this of itself be more than a very mystifying and dramatic end to the biography of Jesus? The essence of the resurrection faith was not, and cannot have been, an opinion as to what happened to Christ's body.

I have spoken of the narratives in the Gospels as *legenda*. But the explicit statement of the apostle Paul cannot be so described. He was writing a letter, not a homily or liturgy. He was writing to the church in Corinth some twenty years or so after the alleged event, and he claims to be stating that which was the common knowledge of the Church. He was seen by Peter, says Paul; then by the twelve. Did he in fact mean by the eleven, with Judas gone, or did this happen after the election of Matthias to take the traitor's place? Then he was seen by more than five hundred brethren, most of whom were still alive and could be cross-questioned if anyone doubted the apostle's word. After that he was seen by James. Last of all, says the apostle, I saw him too. We may claim that this is firsthand, authentic, contemporary evidence. There can be no serious question of the historical fact that all these persons saw, or believed that they had seen, Jesus after his death.

They saw or believed that they had seen. Let us keep for the moment to the testimony of Paul, neglecting the later stories in the Gospels, and let us assume for the moment that what he records was "only a vision," as we say. What reality attaches to a vision? Visions, I submit, may be true or false. The supposition that the visions of the risen Christ were hallucinations of a kind that afflict the sick or mentally deranged does not make sense. It does not make sense for the reason that hallucinations of such a kind cannot possibly account for the faith and witness of the Christian Church. But there are visions which, though we call them "mere visions," may yet be true. Psychologists would agree that more particularly in the case of persons of a certain temperament any profound emotional experience is apt to objectify itself in vision or audition. For instance, when a prophet in the Old Testament says, "The word of the Lord came unto me, saying," it is impossible for us to decide whether he means, as we should say, "I seemed to hear," or whether he did actually suppose himself to hear a voice. What does it matter? When he says, "I saw," it does not in the least matter whether he means, "I seemed to see," or is telling of a real vision. We must take it as a matter of indubitable historical fact that the disciples saw, or seemed to see, the Lord. We are

88

not interested in the modern question whether our ubiquitous photographers, had they been present, could have taken a picture of the appearance. The real question is whether the disciples had a hallucinatory vision of Christ, though he was not there—this would be parallel to the bedroom visions of the sick—or were so utterly seized of his actual living presence with them that this experience objectified itself as a seeing with their eyes. If we have to choose between these alternatives, we must choose the latter by every canon of common sense. I am not asserting as a fact that the vision of Christ was, as we say, "only a vision"; but if it was "only a vision," I say it was a true vision. They did not see Christ although he really was not there; on the contrary, they saw him because really he was there.

This brings me back to my contention that the stories of the resurrection appearances point to a profound religious experience of the first disciples. Of this I would offer two probable illustrations. First, there seems to be an increasing measure of agreement among scholars that behind the Fourth Gospel there lies directly the testimony of an eyewitness. We know that the Lord appeared to Peter. We are not required to doubt the substantial accuracy of that most moving narrative in the Fourth Gospel concerning the Lord's appearance to Peter, the leader, the denier, with its threefold question, "Lovest thou me?" and Peter's brokenhearted answers. If we attempt to imagine the emotions and mental sufferings of Peter during the days following the Crucifixion, when, as we read, he in his despair went back to his fishing, we should suppose that if the Lord did really appear to Peter, it must have been in some such way as this. In other words, the appearance to Peter was not some mere hallucinatory vision of a person whom he had supposed to be dead and who now appeared to be alive; it was, rather, the most touching and intimate personal experience wherein Peter received forgiveness and a new charge, and in fact new life.

My second illustration is an event of which we have in fact three separate accounts in the Acts of the Apostles, namely, the conversion of the apostle Paul. The accounts differ, and it would be very unwise to lay stress on details, but it will not be disputed that his vision took place during his journey to Damascus. We cannot now cross-question the apostle, and perhaps our modern eager questions would be unintelligible to him. But we may properly stress his assertion that his vision of the Lord was parallel to, was one in a series with, the other appearances of the Lord after the Resurrection. Yet we may ask without flippancy how Paul could recognize Jesus if he saw him. There is reference in the stories to a bright light and to the hearing of a voice, but the element of seeing would appear to have been relatively small in this experience. Yet this, as the apostle would give us to understand, was a seeing precisely parallel to the other appearances of the Lord to the disciples. Moreover, it is quite plain that whatever may have been the physical or hallucinatory elements in the vision, it refers to a profound and overwhelming religious experience wherein Paul, the persecutor of the Church, became aware that Jesus, whom he believed to be discredited and dead, was in fact the living Lord, the Saviour.

I hope that I am not unduly laboring a point which is self-evident. Men of the modern world, sincere and not irreligious, who have had a scientific upbringing and have some knowledge of psychology put the question to us in all earnestness: Can we really believe in the Resurrection? We are bound to reply, I think, that there are many questions here, the answers to which wholly elude us for the present, but that by the resurrection stories we understand that these men in a sudden overwhelming experience became aware of the living presence of the Lord who had been crucified, dead, and buried. But I think we should add that no one could feel bound to accept that evidence unless or until he himself had begun to glimpse the realities to which that experience points.

My conclusion so far seems tentative or even negative. The first disciples' message was summed up in the phrase "Jesus and the Resurrection"; but if the Resurrection is an event so obscure to us today, can we put it in the forefront of the Christian message now, can we insist upon it as essential to the Christian faith; is it not inevitably a matter for surmise, for opinion, for suspended judgment? To many historical questions which our interest naturally raises, no clear answer can be given; but from the religious question raised by these stories there is no honorable escape.

The religious question, as I have said, is this: Jesus came into Galilee proclaiming that the hour had struck, that the kingdom of God was at hand; in other words, he proclaimed the imminence of a decisive act of God that should end the present period of world history and introduce another, the age of God. He consistently proclaimed that message; he lived by that faith, and on the very night of his arrest, when his death was unavoidable and his whole cause seemed foundering in disaster, he assured his disciples that in his death was inaugurated a new covenant between God and man, that in his death the decisive intervention of God was being actually accomplished. He died in faith. Was he deceived, or did in fact God intervene, and has the new world dawned? If by the decisive event we have to mean the stars falling from heaven and the moon being literally turned into blood and the end of the world, quite certainly that did not happen. We should be very unwise to suppose that spiritual-minded Jews, and how much more unwise to suppose that Jesus Christ, interpreted the expected decisive catastrophic act of God in external and physical terms like these. The Christian belief in the Resurrection is fundamentally the conviction that Jesus Christ in his expectation of a great creative act of divine intervention was not deceived, that his faith was vindicated, that the power of evil has in principle been broken, and that the new age of God is here. This is the question of the Resurrection, a crucial question upon which every serious man must make up his mind. It is not a matter of proof but of faith. Yet this is not an altogether esoteric belief wholly lacking confirmation in the world without, for we may reasonably ask the secular historian to agree that the coming of Jesus Christ marks the watershed in human history.

What we call the resurrection of Jesus Christ is rooted in history in the sense that something occurred which quite literally turned the course of history. But what precisely was it that occurred? Here we fumble for answers in the presence of the historian. The event was historical in that within a limited time it can be dated. It was not historical but was trans-historical in the sense that apart from revelation, which was of its essence, we cannot assert exactly what it was, and revelation is not a matter with which the historian can conveniently deal. But in some degree we can analyze the revelation. If we consider what we may know or must surmise about the appearance of Jesus to Peter, to Paul, and to the others, we may say first in our clumsy half-technical language that they were suddenly smitten with an overmastering awe and wonder in the realization of God, man's ultimate concern. It is God who is revealed in revelation.

92

But this experience was not like that described by the mystics who claim to be aware of a mystical union with God beyond thought and language, for their experience seems to be that of an All which also is a Nothingness. The experience of the apostles had a clear intellectual content; in its simplest form God had said "Yes" to Jesus. All Christian theology is in fact the attempt to work out the implications of the revelation of God as saying "Yes" to Jesus.

I lay this stress upon what may be called the subjective element in the matter of the Resurrection, because apart from the spiritual illumination of the revelation, the historical events, whatever they were, could not have created the Christian movement. Granted the empty tomb a fact, the empty tomb of itself proves nothing except that the body was no longer where it had been laid. It may be—I am not putting this forward as my own view but as a possibility—that the narratives of the sepulcher are legends in the same sense as the story that on the night of the Crucifixion the departed saints walked again in the city of Jerusalem.

We should all hesitate to take that story as literally true. But take it as a legend and consider what the legend means, the faith behind it. All the powers of sin and darkness had been gathered together against Jesus; they may be summed up in the grim mythological figure of Death. They conspired together and they caught him; he could not escape them; he was killed; he passed the portals of death, and the great gates clanged behind him. What a sigh of relief arose from all the powers that had done him to death! At last they had foiled him; he was dead and done for. But as in the primitive story Samson came out of Gaza carrying the great gates upon his shoulders, so Christ had broken the bars of death, be-

93

cause it was not possible that he should be holden of it, and as he came out he brought the departed with him. Not the mere immortality of the soul is the faith behind this story, but victory, victory over sin and victory over death. We cannot answer the historian's questions with any confidence, but that is the faith of the Resurrection.

> There is a darkness through excess of light
>   Where Time is traversed by Eternity,
> And heavenly vision breaks on mortal sight,
>   Immortal putting on mortality.
>   Such is our darkness and our light when he,
> A Man with men, availed through deadly pain
>   All souls, all ages to procure in fee,
> Who from a transom 'gan his hidden reign,
> The dolour of the world wresting to final gain.[1]

The point of these stories is victory. It is historic in that the victory can be dated; it is trans-historical in that it cannot be treated by the historian as such.

But the Resurrection is not to be sundered from Pentecost. There the outpouring of the Holy Spirit corresponds to palpable historical facts with which the historian must deal; for whatever legendary stories may gather around the Resurrection and Pentecost, there is no shadow of doubt that at this time there entered into the stream of history a new force or power; there appeared a type of person and of society such as had not been known before, and the story of mankind since that date has been very largely the narrative of the impact of that society upon the world.

Who was this man? It may seem that my argument, if it may be called an argument, has been deflected, but this in a way has been inevitable. Let me recapitulate. I said first in this connection that none of those who

[1] From my *The Labyrinth*.

94

saw Jesus of Nazareth doubted for a moment that he was a real man. I asked what manner of man he was and drew my evidence primarily from the contemporary witness of the apostle Paul. It was Jesus who inspired, and who is indirectly depicted in, such passages as the hymn of love in I Cor. 13. I then asked what he did and replied in briefest form that he went about doing good, healing the sick, and seeking the outcasts of society. Then came the question, still a strictly historical question, where within limits a historical answer still seems possible—What did he teach? He proclaimed, I said, the advent of God's kingdom, in effect some decisive act of God. He ventured everything upon this decisive divine intervention which, he said, was to be accomplished through his death. At this point of the argument we inevitably ceased to be dealing with a purely historical question. For, curiously enough, the question whether there was or was not a decisive act of God is not a question which the historian as such can answer. The historian may see that the coming of Jesus marked a turning point in human history, and as a historian he may fail to give a satisfactory account of how it came to be such; but as a historian he does not see in it the act of God. History is concerned with the acts of men, not the *gesta Dei*. It would be only by revelation, by some ecstasy of the reason, that we could apprehend God's vindication of Jesus in the coming of the Holy Spirit and the promise of the final victory in his decisive victory in time.

The subject of the teaching of Jesus seems to have been the nature and coming of the kingdom, not himself; yet of himself he did speak both implicitly and explicitly. If we consider these sayings, forgetting as best we can the traditional doctrines of his person, and putting his words in their historical context, the question inevitably arises. Was he mad? The Jews, his contemporaries, prided themselves above all things in possessing, as they supposed, the law of God; the "yoke of the law" they gladly took upon them; it was their glory. This was the religious tradition in which Jesus of Nazareth was brought up. This, we might say, was his religion. Hear him now say: "Come unto me, all ye that labor and are heavy laden, and I will give you rest. Take my yoke upon you, and learn of me; for I am meek and lowly in heart: and ye shall find rest unto your souls"; and, "It was said by them of old time [in the law of God] . . . but I say unto you. . . ." Are these the sayings of a megalomaniac, a lunatic, or, if not, what is this man? What is this "Son of man," as he calls himself, who declares that he has come to call sinners, that he has come to give his life a ransom for many, who actually asserts that his death will establish a new covenant between Almighty God and man? This all sounds like the sad outpouring of a disordered brain; our asylums show plenty of cases of this kind. But he was not mad. In those last dreadful days of what we call the Passion he alone was calm and serene; he alone did not lose his head. Moreover, psychiatrists and psychotherapists agree, I believe, that one who is himself touched with insanity cannot perform the sort of mental or spiritual healing such as is involved in the stories of the casting out of demons. Here is paradox or antinomy indeed! He says what no sane man could say; yet he was sane if ever man was. The riddle is really insoluble except by some exercise of the ecstatic reason whereby we apprehend, or begin to apprehend, or apprehend in some degree, that what he said was literally true, that he does give rest to the souls of men, that he does in fact call sinners and bring them to God, that his death has in fact ransomed many from the bonds of fear and sin, and that in fact a new age has been inaugurated by his coming, man has moved into a new dispensation under a new covenant made in his name, a new world has been created. I have, I think, said enough to show that what we rather loosely call the doctrine of the divinity of Jesus Christ, however unsatisfactory its traditional forms, is not a mere mystification of the theologians; it represents an attempted answer to facts of history, and experience, so far as we can ascertain them.

We are moving more and more away from the merely historical into the sphere of revelation. By this, however, as you remember, I do not mean the realm of esoteric doctrines supposed to be delivered ready-made from heaven; revelation is a matter of experience. It is on its human side the act of the ecstatic reason whereby through some historical event or situation we become aware of the ultimate Ground of being, of God in his relationship to us men. But the phrase "religious experience" needs some exposition, for it causes disquiet to many, since it has in their ears an esoteric or subjective sound. Each man's experience is proper and private to himself; by no means and under no circumstances can his experience be the experience of another man. One might say, for instance, that when he goes out from a very warm room into very cold air, he experiences a sense of giddiness; that such a man really did have this experience would not be denied by those who would declare that nothing of the kind lay in their own experience. Such experience is purely private, peculiar to the individual, idiosyncratic. But on the other hand, I might say that I experience an extraordinary uplifting of the spirit when I hear Beethoven's *Fifth Symphony*, and you might well say, "Yes, so do I." Under no circumstances could your experiencing be my experiencing, nor will your feelings, thoughts, emotions be identical with mine. Yet we might both use the same phrase, an exaltation of spirit, and each would understand what the other meant. In both cases the experience arises from hearing the same sounds. Here our experience has an objective side no less than a subjective: there is something that we both experience. On its physical side we experience certain waves of sound, whatever those may be. These sound waves are the occasion or the medium of the spirit's exaltation. What, then, is this exaltation of the spirit? It is no doubt a feeling. But we do not mean by it merely an exaltation of sensation, for such a phrase, I think, could bear no meaning. Our "spirit" is somehow our whole person, our mental or spiritual self even more than our physical self. We could not, it may be, define the intellectual content of this experience, yet, though nonconceptual, it is not nonintellectual, for it is with our minds that we comprehend the music. Your hearing may be much more acute than mine, your grasp of the music far more profound, yet in the hearing we share a common physical experience and a common spiritual experience. If in one sense all experience is subjective, in such a case as this it is objective too. It is no doubt true that many persons would hear the *Fifth Symphony* with no emotion other than excessive boredom, but this lamentable fact would not lead you and me to doubt that we had received some spiritual enrichment, that we had glimpsed a world of beauty, of wonder, and of truth through Beethoven, through the score, the orchestra, the waves of sound. We are quite sure that we have not suffered from some purely private autointoxication of the nerves; we have enjoyed a common experience of some spiritual communication.

Religious experience is of this kind. It is at once personal and yet common, subjective and yet objective too;

nonconceptual in form, yet apprehended by the reason. Religious experience, which is the correlative of revelation, is experience of God. Let me illustrate revelation from two mysterious passages in the Old Testament. Revelation came in the Voice

which spoke

To Abraham 'neath Mamre's whispering oak,
Who spurned the cities of the wise Chaldees
Their pomp, their lore, their skyey deities,
Who "staggered not in unbelief," but trod,
Trusting the secret promises of God,
A sojourner, a pilgrim, Canaan's land,
And knew the Presence in the flaming brand
Which 'twixt the sacrificial pieces stole
when the "horror of great darkness" swept his soul.[2]

The other passage is that supreme and really ineffable moment described in Exod. 24:9-11: "Then went up Moses and Aaron, Nadab, and Abihu, and seventy of the elders of Israel; and they saw the God of Israel; and there was under his feet as it were a paved work of a sapphire stone, and as it were the body of heaven in his clearness. And upon the nobles of the children of Israel he laid not his hand; also they saw God, and did eat and drink." How idle to ask exactly what happened! What happened was the founding of the historic religion of Israel, an event so mysterious, so numinous, so tremendous that the thunder of it rolls round the world today and still shakes us with a kind of reverent fear. The resurrection experience which founded the Christian Church must have been like that. Its background was that ghastly torture and judicial murder, and it was the sudden, unexpected, blinding apprehension that God had said "Yes" to Jesus.

Can we define more closely or satisfactorily the Chris-

[2] From my *A Gallimaufry.*

tian revelation? God has revealed himself in many ways, as the writer to the Hebrews says, and in many fragments. The ecstatic apprehension of Beauty is, as I suppose, a revelation of the divine. This, however, has no easily definable intellectual or conceptual content. The revelation to the Hebrew prophets could more readily be put into words, but the words mislead us if we think that by accepting them we have received the revelation. Not many Christians have been so deeply, so overwhelmingly aware of God as were the Hebrew prophets, and we should beware of thinking that Christians are more religious than non-Christians. We are, as I suppose, incomparably less religious than the prophets, and many a Moslem or Hindu may be more religious than many a Christian. But there is plainly a revelation of the divine which comes to Christians through Jesus Christ and does not come through any other medium. To discover this we should look at outstanding examples rather than at the average Christian. There must be very many Christians whose faith hardly can be said to derive from any personal ecstatic apprehension of the divine in awe and wonder. But they are genuine Christians. They have enough religious experience to say "Yes" to the words and witness of those with greater immediate sensitivity to the divine. They say "Yes" because there is in them some inkling, intimation, or dim apprehension of what the saints and prophets say.

There is of course very much in the religious experience of Christians which has its counterpart in other religions. If it were not so, if the alleged Christian revelation contradicted the word of God which saints and seers and prophets and poets and scientists outside Christianity have heard, we should indeed be at a standstill; the realm of nature would be divided by an impassable gulf from the realm of revelation; a dualism intolerable to thought would be introduced into our apprehension of the universe; the world of science and nature, if we were Christians, would no longer be the world of the God of our religion. Yet in the experience of Christians there is an element which is not found elsewhere. Richard Reitzenstein points out somewhere that many or most of the expressions of the New Testament can be paralleled from other religions, but the concept of forgiveness, followed by reconciliation, has no parallel. What is quite new and quite distinctive in the Christian experience is the conviction that Almighty God cares for each individual person, and not least for the outcast and the sinner, that through his own direct action, and at a cost which only the Cross can measure, the individual's sins are forgiven in response to faith, and that the individual is personally reconciled to a personal God. Reconciliation is the keyword of the distinctive experience of Christians. But at once we ask: Could this conceivably be an experience corresponding to reality? The conception that the infinitesimal object which is I should be personally reconciled with Almighty God, maker of heaven and earth, sounds so preposterous that it hardly can be stated in a form that will not make the nonbeliever laugh. Why then do people believe nothing less than this? This preposterous, this incredible belief has come to men quite certainly and solely through the historic Figure about whom we have been asking, Who is this Man?

How does this belief, this experience, come to men through him? He spoke of the love of God for all his creatures; he not only spoke of it, but he also manifested in his life the kind of love of which he spoke. He was not a theologian proclaiming doctrines of the goodness of God and the love of God, but one who in his own person made God's love and presence real to men; that which

101

he said seemed credible when he said it. That, up to a point, we can understand, for we know how a man can carry conviction by the force of his personality and by what he is. He might by these means undoubtedly have persuaded a few people for a short time, only to leave them utterly disillusioned in the end. What was the use of his proclaiming the goodness of God, the care and love of God for all his children, when the facts of his own doom seemed plainly to contradict everything that he had said? I suggested before that he might quite honorably, as we say, have refused the Cross and gone abroad or into some retirement. Speculative history is in general a sad waste of time, but this much we may say— had he died in his bed, to use our expression, then if his teaching were remembered at all, he would have left behind him after his death a happy doctrine of God's kindness and providence, which we should reject for precisely the reasons which lead us to reject as sentimental and unrealistic the easy optimism of the nineteenth century. A very pretty doctrine, we should say, and how nice it would be if it were only true, but unfortunately the world is constructed on other lines. We might perhaps still accept as a theory the view that behind phenomena there may be a Being who should be regarded, at least by the fortunate, as a benign Providence, our Well-wisher, but for a gospel of an agonizing, redeeming love extended to the least and worst, there would be no basis whatsoever.

Had Jesus of Nazareth taken the way of escaping from the Cross, we should have said of him, if we had heard of him, that he was a lover of his fellows; he was very kind to them; he loved them genuinely up to a point, but not utterly and unconquerably; for when it was plain that they rejected him, he made the best of it and retired into obscurity. But in fact, "having loved his own, . . . he loved them unto the end"; he could not leave them; rather than leave them he would love them through all the horror of what they could do, the rejection, the crown of thorns, the spitting, and the Crucifixion; almost his last words are said to have been a prayer for their forgiveness. It is through this death that men by revelation or by an exercise of the ecstatic reason have claimed to apprehend that the Being who is the ultimate Ground of existence is love in the awful sense of a love unbreakable and all-embracing; it has been said of Jesus that with arms outstretched upon the Cross "he espoused to himself the soul of every man, for better for worse, for richer for poorer, and death never should them part," and in that love and utter self-giving, in that revelational event, men have apprehended the Word of God himself, through that event they have been brought home to God, they have been reconciled with God.

Upon this only two comments will be in place, first, that had it not been for the Resurrection, that is, for the conviction and assurance that God himself had vindicated Jesus, the Cross would have been the final proof not of the presence of God in history but of the absence of God from history. The love of Jesus for mankind is not the love of God unless God vindicated Jesus; but if God vindicated Jesus, the love of Jesus is the revelation of the mind of God. That is the issue of the Resurrection. Second, if the Man of Nazareth not only spoke of this love of God for men but was himself this very love incarnate, and so has reconciled men to God, who was this Man?

There have been many answers to this question. The Jewish Christians said he was Messiah; by this somewhat vague but magnificent symbol they attempted to express his significance for God and man. Perhaps we can do no better in the end; but this was a Jewish term that could mean little outside Jewish circles. He was the Word of God, the Logos, the Word of God made flesh, said others. That was a more philosophical and more universal term, and as such, more satisfactory, but again it is a symbol rather than an explanation, for what can be literally meant by "the Word of God made flesh"? Paul spoke of Jesus as the second Adam, the head of a new humanity; I shall come back to this conception; it is useful, but it tells us what he is rather than who he is. Many theories of his person have been adumbrated through the centuries, but none is more illuminating and none more ultimately unsatisfactory than the doctrine which deserves the name of classical. Let me interpret it to you in my own words rather than in the traditional language of Greek metaphysics. It comes to this, I think: all human beings have the same psychophysical organism in virtue of which they are human beings; the Greeks called this man's "nature"; it was the same in all men everywhere. Jesus Christ, as this doctrine maintains, wholly and entirely shared with us this psychophysical organism. It was his as it is ours. But every man has, in addition to that common psychophysical organism which is identical in all men, that which makes him a distinct individual, Peter or Paul or John; he has his own private and ultimate center of consciousness, his own ego. When we interrogate or cross-question ourselves about this our own deepest personal individual nature, we are conscious of our creatureliness and of our sinfulness or imperfection. We are aware of ourselves, in fact, as created beings dependent for our being upon that which is not ourselves, and as sinners. But Jesus, according to this theory, while he shared our common human nature, so far as concerns his psychophysical organism, was at the center of his being, in his ultimate individuality, in his ego, not a sinful created being but the Word of God. I am not sure that this theory is really intelligible; at least it breaks down when we try to analyze it; I am very far indeed from suggesting, as some ecclesiastics do, that you should believe this to be an accurate statement of the facts, but it does express with great clarity and precision the kind of assertions which the facts of history and experience seem to require us to make about Jesus of Nazareth. It is, if I may presume to say so, an extremely ingenious putting of the case; it is a remarkable attempt to express the mystery of the person of Jesus.

But here I have run into a very great difficulty which I must not avoid or try to hide. A presupposition of the Church's Christology has been an explicit doctrine of the sinlessness of Jesus. Let us very frankly admit that we cannot hope to prove a negative of that kind. Let us further admit that we cannot prove against all possible cavil that he is sinless as depicted in the Gospels. The most we could possibly demonstrate would be that nothing in the Gospels is inconsistent with his sinlessness. I think I do not know what sinlessness or faultlessness would mean. But there is no escaping from the mystery of his person. I have raised the question why we do not reject him pityingly as a megalomaniac and a madman. Christians cannot do that because of what he has been to the souls of men, because his coming has been in some mysterious way the coming of God himself to men, because through him there has been a decisive act of God which has wrested history from its ancient course and opened to all men a new world of grace. Hence the traditional orthodox doctrine that he is both very Man and very God. But what does that mean? Is it really intelligible? Can it be conceived? I submit to you that if he was as he is described in the Gospels and epistles of the New Testament, if he has been to men that which Christian experience alleges, if in some indefinable sense his coming is the coming of God to men, we could never have a satisfactory theory of his person. If by a doctrine of the person of Christ we mean a theory that will explain his person, it is from the nature of the case impossible. The idea of the God-man, however inevitable it may be, is in itself but a symbol; it is not a fully intelligible notion.

But that does not mean that we should cease to think about his relationship to God and man; we cannot abandon ourselves to the irrational, and that which is indefinable is not of necessity indefinite. We must, if we can, find terms or categories which will make his figure real to us as we read the records in the Gospels. I have myself received most light here from my friend, Donald Baillie of St. Andrews, but let me put the matter in my own words, only observing that I am trying not to prove anything, but only to present this enigmatic figure in some way conceivable to Christians. When I was at school, we used to rely greatly upon a book, of which I still retain a copy, entitled *Carey's Gradus*:

> *Saepe perlegi incassum*
> *Carey's Gradus ad Parnassum.*

This book—though it often failed to carry me up to Parnassus—was designed to help us with our Latin verses. I am not sure how far authority approved of it, but we scarcely could have survived without it. It gave us synonyms, epithets, and specimen lines from the classical poets. I could imagine, though to the best of my recol-

106

lection this never actually occurred, my form master saying to me, "That was a very good copy of verses you did for me last night," and I might reply, "Oh, no, Sir, that was Carey really!" I should not have meant that I did not in fact compose the lines, but I should mean that the credit for them, the merit of them, their excellence, was really due not to any poetic inspiration of my own but to the suggestion and inspirations of another. I did those lines; yet in some real sense it was Carey, not I, who did them. That imagined situation represents a largely external relationship between two persons. A much more intimate relationship is possible. I might see a schoolboy and say, "Is that young Doe? I remember him as a happy-go-lucky scalawag, and now he seems a responsible and conscientious member of society"; and you might reply, "That's all due to our friend Roe, his schoolmaster; he has been a different person since he has been under him." The reference here is to that mysterious event or state called "influence," a metaphor but most appropriate; it indicates how in some strange way the life or outlook or character of one man may flow into, that is, influence, another's. This we can by no means explain, though we all know that it happens. Personality is not something with a steel casing around it, as it were; it is porous. It is a paradox, of which we are all aware, that a man never ceases to be himself, yet under the influence of another he becomes somebody quite different from what he was before. A young man, let us say, falls under the influence, the spell, of Albert Schweitzer; he gives up remarkable prospects at home and goes as a doctor to serve in Africa. We say, "It is Albert Schweitzer over again." We do not mean that in a literal sense. The young man remains himself; the desiring, the planning, the decisions were all

107

his own; yet anyone can see that but for Albert Schweitzer his life would have been drawn along very different lines.

I labor an obvious point, but let the notion be extended to religion. When Paul says, "It is no longer I that live, but Christ liveth in me" (A.S.V.), he certainly did not mean that he had ceased to be Paul of Tarsus, that he could no longer properly use the first person singular in speaking of himself. What he must mean is that his thoughts, his feelings, and his plans were now due to the conscious influence upon his life, the inflowing into his life, of the life of Jesus Christ. The phrase is fully intelligible to us, however far the experience may be from ours. Yet even we in some small measure know from our own experience what he meant. There was, for instance, an occasion when you very nearly made a bad mistake; you were going to give a man what he deserved, you said; you were going, in fact, to make a bad situation worse; but in a flash you saw the situation with new eyes; you saw what you ought to do or say, and with a sudden decision you acted on this impulse, this insight, and the situation was saved; indeed it was redeemed. "I was just going to do this and that," you said afterward, "when by the grace of God I realized just in time what I must do." Such an experience may be rare and intermittent with us, but we have known people (saints we call them) who are under the influence of Christ to such a degree that the apostle's words, "it is no longer I that live, but Christ liveth in me," sound natural and appropriate in their case. And when these Christlike people do anything, it is really Christ doing it in them. This is no doubt most mysterious, but I keep close to the facts of our experience.

I come back to the person of Jesus of Nazareth. It is written of him in the Fourth Gospel that "the Son can

do nothing of himself, but what he seeth the Father do."
It was as if he saw God healing the crippled man, so he
stretched forth his hand and bade him take up his bed
and walk. It was God who cured the sick man. Jesus
insisted upon that; but it was Jesus who, as we say, performed the miracle. Jesus did not cease to be himself
when he so acted, yet it was God who acted through
him. To the testimony of the Fourth Gospel we might
add a text of our own: "The Son sayeth nothing of himself, but what he heareth the Father say." It was as if
Jesus heard God say to the rich young ruler, "Sell all
that thou hast"; therefore he said it. He, Jesus, said it, but
it was God who spoke through him.

I suspect that there are many persons—not ministers
only—who could say in wonder and in all sincerity and
in great humility, "There have been occasions in my life
when God spoke to a man through me or when God
acted through me." With most of us such occasions are
sadly rare and intermittent; but whereas we can speak and
act like that sometimes, Jesus of Nazareth seems to
Christians to have spoken and acted always like that.
His communion with God was uninterrupted; his words
were the words of God, his acts the acts of God. I have
here in mind, of course, his deeds and words toward
man. I do not mean that when he closed his eyes and
went to sleep, it was God who closed his eyes and went
to sleep, that when he ate his breakfast, it was God who
had breakfast, that when he prayed, his prayers were to
himself. That sort of idea, which, less crudely expressed,
has been very common, indeed traditional, in the Church,
seems to me really inconsistent with the plain and obvious
fact that no one doubted that he was a real man. But
in all his ministry his words to men were God's words,
his deeds God's deeds, so that not sometimes but always
he could say, "Not I but the grace of God" or "Not I

but the Spirit of God that dwelleth in me." So conscious was he of this that he could in fact say "I"—"But I say unto you . . . and I will give you rest." In saying this I am explaining nothing, I am offering no alternative doctrine of his person; but I am attempting to put before you what to Christians he seems to have been in terms not so remote from our own experience as to be unintelligible to us.

But the mystery is deeper than I here suggest. We may not doubt that when Jesus was an infant, he was a real infant and subject to all the limitations of an infant; when he was a boy, he was a real boy who played weddings and funerals with his companions, as one of his parables suggests, and who in the carpenter's shop when the hammer slipped in his fingers, "learned by the things that he suffered," as all of us must learn. But there is nothing in the stories to suggest that he came to God through inward struggle, that he went through those periods of purgation and illumination before union with God, a process made familiar to us by the writings of the mystics, that he was conscious of alienation from God through sin. He seems to have been *arrivé*, as the French say, from the beginning. Here indeed are negatives which cannot be proved. But there can be no doubt that there is a supreme mystery about his person.

It is the traditional doctrine of the Church that he is both God and Man, and theologians have attempted to give some account of the God-man. All their constructions seem to me to be open to grave objection and to be unintelligible in the end. I have no theory to substitute for theirs. But we understand Paul when he says, "It is no longer I that live, but Christ liveth in me," and we do not ask how anybody can be both Paul and Christ, for we know from experience that one person can indwell another without destruction of the

110

other's personality. When we try to describe what Jesus of Nazareth was, it seems necessary to say that the indwelling of the Spirit of God, which in us is so partial, intermittent, and imperfect, was in him whole, continual, and complete. He was himself, but he was the Spirit of God incarnate, he was God himself made manifest in a human life.

5

The Cosmic Christ

I turn from what we may call the doctrine of Christ's person to the doctrine of redemption. There have been many doctrines of the Atonement. None of them is, so to say, official, except in certain small segments of the Church. Many of them seem to us absurd, even grotesque; but we misjudge them unless we realize what it is that they are seeking to explain. There are Anselm's famous words in *Cur Deus Homo*, where he says, *Nondum considerasti quanti ponderis sit peccatum* —"Thou hast not yet considered how great is the weight of sin." I suspect that much which is said and written by Christians about sin should be reckoned morbid, but we may consider for a moment the weight of sin.

How often do we give thanks for the peace and beauty of our countryside? What a world in which men should live happily and till the ground and be truly human! I could believe that all people in all countries feel as much about their fatherland. And how much good will there is in the world, and how little on the whole is the ill will! Where shall we find anyone desiring war? Yet we live under the constant threat of a war so awful, so universal, so destructive as would lay

112

waste in unimaginable horror this fair world, and might even destroy this planet. It might be thought that in a world so beautiful, so rich, so varied as this, all men should be happy. But are people happy? In our civilization the motion-picture theaters, the radio and television are distractions of our unhappiness rather than contributions to our happiness. Are there not broken homes innumerable in the world, millions who are permanently hungry, millions who are slaves in labor camps or prisons? There seems an utter dissonance between the beauty of the world, the goodness of human nature, the yearnings of men on the one side and on the other slums, slavery, destitution, frustration, and appalling boredom. I remember the lovely spring of 1944 when I sat in my garden among the jonquils, as you call them, and watched the butterflies, and was interrupted every few minutes by the roar of bombers overhead:

A June-hot sun in April's cloudless sky,
　The trees in bud, the ancient College mound
　　With primrose and narcissus gay, the ground
With daisies carpeted, a butterfly
Proving her wings—see jocund Nature lie
　Youthful in loveliness by wooing sound
　　Of song-birds lulled, but circling all around
In the higher heavens bombers and gliders ply.

So great a peace in 'midst of so great ills,
　Such gladness on the edge of direst woe!
　　My heart divided 'twixt a deep content
And anguish! O'er the springing daffodills
　Perfected engines of destruction go,
　　Primed for the invasion of a Continent.

These planes were manned by those who hated war,

loved home, were wonderfully kind to children, and they were off to perform deeds of unimaginable horror on the Continent. Their operation was not their sin, but it was sin. This contrast between what is and what so clearly ought to be is heightened the more man is aware of the goodness, the providence, the love of God. This madness, this evil, this sin seems indeed a demonic force, far greater, far more ineradicable than the petty sins of little people. Yet we may do well to think that wars come from tempers not unlike ours, from impatiences like ours, from misunderstandings, failures to see another's point of view, lack of imagination, lack of caring for the remoter consequences of action. Whoever set out to build slums? They were not built out of malice, but because men did not think, did not care, did not exercise imagination, did not love. We are all caught up in this network of iniquity, swept along by this demonic force, and the suffering of men and women and innocent children is beyond imagination. What is the use of ingeminating peace and begging everybody to be nice and kind? Can we conceive of God as venerable and remote, advising his helpless children to be nice, and himself utterly ineffective to help them in their agony? It seems to me to stand to reason that the goodness of God, if God be good, must be an effective goodness. It must be an effectual goodness in respect not only of individual men but also of the whole order of his appointing.

Let me speak first of his effectual action in respect of individuals. I have pointed to the cross and resurrection of Jesus as a revelatory event. We may think but poorly of the theological interpretations and theories of the past, but it remains that men through the ages have been convinced that by the Cross God has dealt radically with evil, that he has acted decisively with regard

to it, that the Cross is not merely the dreadful manifestation of the sin of man but is also the revelation of
the redeeming love of God. The gospel has never been
the abstract assertion that God is love; it has been the
proclamation that God "hath visited and redeemed his
people." This gospel has been corroborated in experience. Those who by ecstatic reason have apprehended
in the Cross a radical divine dealing with evil have
known in experience that evil has been dealt with in
their own lives.

> He breaks the power of canceled sin,
>   He sets the prisoner free;
> His blood can make the foulest clean;
>   His blood availed for me.

This stanza by Charles Wesley obviously expresses his
own deep, personal experience, and its form marks it
as coming from the Evangelical Revival, but in substance it is the experience to which every age of Christian history bears witness, and every race and class.
  It was taught by Anselm that Christ paid for us our
debt to God's offended majesty, as if sin were a kind of
debt which could be paid off for us, that the sacrifice of
Christ sufficed for the debt of all mankind, but would
in fact avail to save only enough persons to make up
the number of the fallen angels. How utterly remote
this is from our way of thinking, and to what devastat-
ing criticism it is open! But when we overhear Anselm
at his prayers, of which some have been recorded for us,
these crude theories we find to have dropped away, and
he cries out in the same ecstasy as Charles Wesley,
whose words I have just cited. The so-called "substitu-
tionary" doctrine of the Atonement was generally
taught a generation or two ago in the Protestantism we

know best and is still insisted on by many. That too seems to me to be open to annihilating criticism, but because it points to the saving fact, it still lifts men from the gutter. We may rightly be critical of all these theories, but the mission work of the Church both at home and abroad produces evidence not to be gainsaid that the name of Jesus "has still its ancient power." He seems to save, if I may so put it, with bad theology, even with almost none. I well remember asking a missionary in India what some once outcast woman, uneducated and bending all day over the paddy fields under the blazing sun, could understand of the Christian religion. "She understands," he replied, "that Christ is stronger than the demons." She would have been somewhat perplexed, I imagine, by Charles Wesley's hymn, but she knew well from her own experience that "he sets the prisoner free." For my part I find here almost insupportable mystery, but I find it quite impossible to believe that this constant victory of Christ over the hearts and lives of millions through the centuries is all mirage and self-deception. No one, I am sure, could take that view if he had looked honestly at the facts of history.

There has been a redemption or salvation or new creation or rebirth of countless individuals through that which they have apprehended through the cross of Christ. But can we say that there has been a victory over evil at large, such as might be called a decisive act of God? In the century of two world wars and of the atomic bomb, of the slaughter of six million Jews in the charnel houses of Germany, of the twelve million slaves in the labor camps of Russia, of more broken homes in North America and Britain than can be counted, can it possibly be said that evil in principle has been overcome by the Cross and Resurrection? Would

116

not a sober judgment be that though undoubtedly Jesus has brought wonderful blessing to many individuals, yet as would-be Saviour of the world he is a failure?

Here we are certainly in the realm of faith or insight, not of proof. There is no quantitative weighing of success and failure, and the story is not ended yet. Shortly after World War II a Dutch friend told me that in 1940, once the Battle of Britain had been won, thoughtful people in Holland were convinced that Germany could not win the war, that Germany in principle was beaten; there might be long and terrible years of endurance before the final victory; they themselves might very probably not live to see their country delivered from the oppressor, but the final result was certain. They believed in ultimate victory by a rational faith, but only the event could vindicate or negate their faith.

John Oman remarks somewhere that while man makes canals that go on a direct and unwavering course till they reach their goal, God made the rivers which meander through devious and slow ways to meet the sea. Often in times of trouble have men been buoyed up by apocalyptic hopes, expecting some immediate divine intervention, but the ways of Providence are like the rivers. There have indeed been spectacular events, such, for instance, as the conversion of savage tribes in a generation into alert and responsible Christian communities as in some of the South Sea Islands or Uganda. But in general, progress, if progress is the word, has been much slower. I remember reading *The Golden Ass* of Apuleius and immediately thereafter *Don Quixote* by Cervantes. Both tell of marvelous travels in a wild and desolate part of Europe, but I thought to myself that if we compare the background of Apuleius' thought with the presuppositions of the Knight of the Sorrowful Countenance and of his faithful servant Sancho Panza, we have

117

some insight into what Christ has done for Europe. Europe has been but imperfectly Christianized, and the Romanism which is the form in which it has largely accepted Christianity has itself been tinged with paganism, but at least we may say that the *mater deum*, the lascivious mother of the gods, has gone, and in her place has come the *mater Dei*, the stainless cult of the Virgin Mary. As a Protestant theologian I am very critical of this new cult, but the change is at least like that from darkness into light.

Moreover, this is an issue where an impartial and objective judgment is peculiarly difficult for us. In North America and Britain we are painfully aware of evil and of godlessness and of secularism; we are apt to forget how much good there is. Apart from the Bible, our peoples have had no history; as nations we owe our very existence to the gospel. It is perhaps only those who for a while have lived in a heathen country who can realize in how deep a sense Christ has shaped the very conventions and background and unconsciously accepted principles which make our countries part of Christendom, though the number of devoted Christians in them may be relatively few. There are many men among us of high ideals and noble character who never go to church and call themselves agnostics, but as a mere matter of history owe everything to Christ.

Communism today represents itself as an atheist faith or science; it will stamp out all religion if it can; it is the implacable foe of Christianity or of any religion. To us it stands for tyranny, Russian imperialism, spiritual and physical oppression, the denial of all the spiritual values of the West. In communism of this kind or in this aspect, in the economic theories of Karl Marx or his bourgeois materialism I have nothing to commend. Communism of this kind is so ugly as to be universally unattractive to all who do not directly profit by it. But the communism of Karl Marx has served itself heir in many parts of the world to the most remarkable spiritual movement of our times. Nothing, it may be, could be more cynical than the communism of the Kremlin, but the so-called "communism" which makes an immense appeal to millions in Asia, in Africa, and indeed to many not ignoble but disillusioned minds elsewhere, is a passionate idealism. Its appeal is spiritual; it proclaims an end to the imperialism of the white races; it knows no color bar; it speaks of a new order of society in which there shall be no privilege of birth or of wealth, in which all social organization shall be for the equal benefit of all, in which, it is anticipated, poverty, hunger, and insecurity shall no longer afflict the common man; it offers hope to the millions of Africa and Asia. There is no essential connection between these hopes and these ideals on the one side and Russian imperialism on the other; indeed, they are in practice incompatibles. It is tragic that this great awakening, this new hope which comes with the compelling power of a religion, should be linked in the minds of millions with the somewhat outmoded economics and the superficial materialism of Karl Marx. These hopes, these ideals, should have been connected with Christianity, for it is historically through the Bible that they came into the world. We are perhaps apt to denounce this type of communism as revolutionary and utopian much as the Reformers denounced Anabaptism long ago. This is too large a theme for me here. Our statesmen have to deal with an international situation that is full of danger, uncertainty, and menace. They must, as best they can, defend and vindicate the spiritual values of the West, and we, Christians though we be, must play our part in the political field according to such wisdom as may be given us. But in the last resort history is in the hands of God, not of the statesmen or dictators. If we read the papers we can learn what man is doing, but it is not given us yet to see what God is doing in and through the turmoil of our time.

Let me sum my argument in brief. I have asked whether we should say that Jesus Christ as Saviour of the world has proved a failure. I said that God makes the winding rivers; it is man who makes canals. The acceptance of Christianity as the official religion of the Roman Empire in the fourth century of our era seemed a marvelous victory for the Cross. A few years later Attila sacked Rome, the barbarians flooded the empire, and Europe entered the Dark Ages, as we call them; but out of the Dark Ages by the providence of God and in his time came Christendom, another triumph, though again a partial triumph, of the Cross. The world of Christendom is at this time in process of dissolution; it is possible enough that another Dark Age lies before mankind; Asia and Africa are awakening and determined to throw off the domination of the West; Russia is in the grip of a secular messianism that would throw the world into revolution and subject it to tyranny; atomic warfare menaces the nations. No wonder men's hearts are failing them for fear! On the other side, through scientific knowledge, which is the outgrowth of Christendom, there lies to man's hand the possibility of a better life for all men on this planet than ever entered into the heart of previous ages to imagine; there is a real deepening of religion within the Christian Church, and there is surging in the hearts of men in every continent a great spiritual longing and a great determination that there shall be a new world order, juster, happier, far more Christian—though that is our word, not theirs—than anything mankind has ever known, and these ideals come from Christ. Both the nearer future and the farther are wholly unpredictable by us. We may claim, however, as rational men, that if the universe as a whole be rational, which is the pre-supposition of scientists, it must be rational in all its parts; there must be a meaning in history, a purpose in the universe to which all its parts contribute. That we ourselves must walk in the ways of love and duty, so far as our blind eyes will guide us, we know well; we must leave the rest in faith. It is much too soon to say that Christ has failed in history as the Saviour of the world, for the story is still in the telling.

But I find very partial satisfaction in this argument, though, as far as it goes, it holds. It is reasonable to have faith that through the tangled coil of our days God "by the tranquil operation of his perpetual Providence" is carrying out the work of man's salvation. It is an assured fact that Jesus of Nazareth has brought deliverance to multitudes of individuals, but the purpose of the universe must lie beyond the universe itself, and the purpose of history must lie beyond the devious course of history. It is quite certain that human history will end some day. It might come, I suppose, by our own folly and presumption in atomic warfare; it must come in any case with the cooling of our planet and the dying of our sun. Shall Jesus then be shown to be the Saviour of the world?

It ill becomes us here to dogmatize. This is the sphere of faith and hope, not of proof and compelling argument. At most we might claim a reasonable faith, a hope that is not groundless. Perhaps hope is ineradicable from man, or at least, when all hope dies, then man himself is spiritually dead. We have been taught by a distinguished French philosopher, Gabriel Marcel, to distinguish between hope in the absolute sense and hope for

121

anything particular. Under normal circumstances a man hopes for this or that, but in a situation that appears desperate, where he cannot see what to hope for, he still hopes. This is hope in the absolute sense. The thought of God may be far away, but ultimately this absolute hope is an implicit prayer to God. Because in spite of all the embranglements and perils and confusion of our age, it is still reasonable to hope; the faith that in the end the providence of God will be found to have been working through the turmoil of the time is a not unreasonable faith.

3. But I come back to theology and the Christian claim that Jesus is the Saviour of the world. In the West theologians have been so obsessed with the matter of sin, so much concerned with the question of who will get to heaven and how large a portion of mankind have only hell to which they may look forward, that the Christian religion has assumed an almost incredibly individualistic form. Let every man save his own soul if by the grace of God he can; the devil undoubtedly will take the hindmost. The salvation of mankind as a whole, as a corporate body, has been but little considered. But Eastern Christian theology has taken seriously that apprehension or intuition of the early Church that God in Jesus, who is God manifest in the flesh, has taken our nature upon him, that in being made man he was made one with all men, that God in his infinite mercy has identified himself for all eternity with all humanity. I would take their hint and develop this idea in my own way and in modern terms.

I may start from the French philosopher-poet-socialist, Charles Péguy, who was killed in World War I, and to whose writings the young men of France turned for hope and comfort in the dark days of their country's capitulation and oppression in World War II. Profoundly Christian in heart and faith, Péguy lived nearly all his days unreconciled to his church. He longed to go to Mass, but the church forbade his comrades to come, threatening them with hell fire; therefore he would not go to Mass if they were kept away, whose need was as great as his. He could not believe that we can be saved in isolation from our brethren. "We must be saved together; we must come to God together," he said. "What would God say to us if we came alone before him? Would he not say, 'Where are the others?'"

I am not sure whether psychologists and philosophers will allow us to say that humanity is some sort of psychic continuum, but I am sure that humanity is some sort of spiritual continuum or, if the phrase offend, a partnership. The old atomic, individualistic conception of human nature must be abandoned; we are persons, not mere individuals. A family lives a common life which not merely binds together the present generation but links them with past and future generations. Neighborhood, whether in living or working, is a less close unity, but we cannot be quit of the influence of our companions and of society upon us. We should not be ourselves apart from other people. The national name we bear, whether American or British, is no mere fortuitous name which many happen in the course of time to share; it points to a common spiritual inheritance which inspires or qualifies all our thinking and gives us the presuppositions of our social life. Nor are we uninfluenced, in spite of iron curtains, by the thoughts, the habits, the aspirations of all other nations. We today are feelingly aware, as previous generations could not be, that humanity is in some sense a unity, a fellowship of coinherence. This mutual influence may be called a fact of nature.

But when we consider love, we are in the sphere of

the conscious and perhaps of the religious. The story is told of some old Gothic warrior who, coming forward for Christian baptism with his followers, asked the officiating priest, "Where are my fathers?" The priest replied regretfully but without hesitation that his fathers, being unbelievers, were in hell. The warrior drew back from the laver saying, "Then I will be gathered to my fathers." He may be deemed to have had far more spiritual insight than many theologians past and present. It is difficult to conceive of any son enjoying the bliss of heaven while he knew his father to be in hell. Jesus told the parable of the shepherd who having the ninety and nine sheep safely in the fold would go out after the one lost sheep "until he find it." The shepherd instinct which was in the heart of Jesus we must believe to be in the heart of God. It may be permissible to say that Jesus came not to save individuals but to save humanity. We should consider the notion unfamiliar in the West but often suggested in the East that the body of Christ is really humanity itself.

It is a trite saying that there is no one but has had somebody to love him. Human love such as that between parents and their children is so strong that it seems to us a breach in nature when it fails; but, says the psalmist, "When my father and my mother forsake me, then the Lord will take me up." In principle Jesus Christ grappled to himself the souls of all men; in principle he died for all; he manifested and made credible the divine love from which none can be excluded; in him, we may say, God identified himself with all humanity, not in the mass but as individuals tied together in the bundle of life and the bonds of mutual affection.

From this we may not draw the easy and too-quick conclusion that in this case all men must be saved, there is no hell, and there was no necessity that Christ should

124

die for us. The so-called "larger hope," which virtually repudiated hell and judgment because of God's alleged good will toward us, was a sentimentalized religiosity quite out of touch with the religion of the Bible, or indeed with any moral seriousness at all. Without judgment, said Calvin, there can be no God. The old descriptions of hell taken literally, as they seem to have been intended, are quite incredible to us today; but our eyes cannot be wholly blind to the awful, the unspeakable sufferings involved in sin, not merely for the victims of sin but even more for the perpetrators when they see what they have done. "They shall look on him whom they pierced." Paul was forgiven for breathing out threatening and slaughter against the Church, for persecuting the saints, for consenting to Stephen's lynching; but did he ever forgive himself? He might be forgiven, yet there could be no ultimate peace for him till he should see how God out of evil brought yet greater good, till under a sense of the mystery of redemption he could have cried, *O felix culpa*—"O blessed fault through which God wrought such good!" We should have some idea of the wages of sin today. We may have some very dim idea of the cost of our redemption, for it was in fact the cross of Jesus Christ which as a matter of history alone made possible the new life, the new humanity, the reconciliation, the working of the Holy Spirit which followed in the world. We may see in Jesus Christ a limitless love that in the end will not be defeated. It should come to us with a shock of surprise that for long centuries in the West men seem to have thought that the work of the Incarnation was to be completed in the relatively small number of individual human beings who, having had the good fortune to have heard of Jesus Christ, or to have been baptized in his name or to have the minimum of necessary saving faith, should alone be ultimately saved. The perspective here is far too small, far too parochial.

It should be impossible for us today. There was a time in Western Christendom when, apart from the hated and persecuted Jews, almost everyone had been baptized and everyone was aware of the Christian religion and the requirements of the Church. Of the millions of India, of China, of Africa men were quite unaware. There were indeed the Moslems battering at the gates of Europe; they with their false prophet would as enemies of the Cross find themselves in due time in hell; it was a pity, but no doubt it was their fault, and it occurred in the inscrutable providence of God. Moslems were not personally and individually known; they could be consigned to hell without any feelings of personal dislike. For practical purposes the world was Christendom, in which everyone had been baptized, and baptism was a powerful and efficacious rite, and though no doubt men would go to hell if they died in mortal sin, it was never too late to repent, and it was possible to hope even for the worst of men that by baptism and some last-minute repentance and the kindly ministrations of the Church they would escape the pains of hell at last. In other words, the relation of the Incarnation to humanity as a whole was not a burning question. The discovery of the New World enlarged men's horizons, but it was possible to think of the New World as an extension of the sphere of Christendom.

Today we are perforce world conscious and aware that Christendom in the old form is no more; we meet constantly in business or in social life those who are not baptized, who have no connection with the Church, and whose lives are bound up with ours. Go into any of your superstores and consider with the eye of a geog-

rapher and a Christian the groceries and provisions that
are there spread out before you—coffee from Brazil,
rice from India, tea from China; why, the whole world
has been laid under contribution that you may do your
shopping and enjoy in health and comfort the life of
your astonishing civilization. The Chinese coolies who
have brought the precious tea leaves to the coast, the
poor women who spend their laborious and burning
days bending over the paddy fields that rice may come
to you, the still half-savage laborers in Brazil, are they
to spend their days laboring for us and to spend eternity in hell because they have never heard the name of
Jesus, while we are to enjoy the profit of their labors
here and the bliss of heaven hereafter? The thought is,
I am sure, intolerable to you once it is presented to you.
In this connection let me observe in passing that it
seems to me a strange and unfortunate thing in these
days most of all that in some churches when the Apostles' Creed is recited, the people omit the clause "he
descended into hell," which symbolizes the preaching
of Christ to those who died in ignorance of his saving
name. The relation of the Incarnation to humanity as
a whole is now an urgent question; we should consider
afresh what the fathers meant when they said that the
Son of God took our human nature on him and identified himself with all humanity. Do we suppose that a
wrong done to an unbeliever is not a wrong done to
Christ himself? Inasmuch as we have refused a cup of
cold water or refused bare political justice to any class
or any people, have we not done it unto him? This
tortured, agonized, and suffering humanity is the body
of the Crucified. But if he is one with all mankind
in our sufferings, shall not all mankind participate in
his redemption in the consummation, when he shall
see of the travail of his soul and shall be satisfied?

Before the time of Copernicus, though the world might seem very large, as men then judged size, the universe was a very limited space; the heavens revolved above the earth like the lid of a vast tureen; God might be conceived as beyond the clouds, but the clouds, after all, are not so very far away, and often they come down low. Today we are all more or less aware of the universe as revealed or imagined by the astrophysicists; we have heard of light-years and of such distances and speeds that we are like to suffer from a permanent vertigo. Our universe is but a mite in an inconceivable world of universes. We do not question what the men of science say, but much of our theology remains to this day on the pre-Copernican scale.

But we must not allow the very large facts which the scientists surmise to make us question the very small facts that we know; we must not permit the illimitable spaces and unimaginable periods to blind our eyes to our true certainties. Yet we must relate our assurances to this vast background. We must not deny that out of the silence and out of the infinities the living God has spoken, just because we are overwhelmed by the wonder and mystery of what we say.

> It is a thing most wonderful,
>   Almost too wonderful to be,
> That God's own Son should come from heaven
>   And die to save a child like me.[1]

It is a thing so wonderful that we certainly should not be surprised that many men brought up in the modern sciences turn from it as a childish fancy; it is a faith that shatters reason, and yet, as I suppose, it is itself the only reason.

[1] Mrs. Alexander.

Out of the silence of the infinities
   There comes a word, though we be slow to hear
And muddy-minded, God to Socrates,
   To Zeno, aye, to every heart sincere
   And low has spoken, drawing wondrous near
In some felt Presence beyond mortal thought,
   Not to be told in language strict and clear,
Misstated in all doctrines men have taught,
Shown in the power whereby their dazzling deeds were
     wrought.

Who the eye planted, shall himself not see?
   Who framed the snowflake, shall not he delight,
The Artist in his handicraft and be
   The Lover of his beauty? In his sight
   Is man but neutral-tinted, composite
Of divers chemicals? Ah, should God care
   And count man worthier than the heavens by right
Of Reason and Desire, how may we dare
Conceive his love or its o'erwhelming instance bear?

But here, Theophilus, falters and dies
   My tremulous song, for Love divine must be
Equal to Power and Wisdom past surmise
   Or understanding. I in silency
   Of awe and wonder stand. For Reason's plea
And Reason's very self were overthrown
   Were there no Son of God, no Calvary.
Amid the half-truths him the Truth I own
Who spake, who was, thy Word, O God not unbeknown.[1]

If our Western theology has been parochial, we may
remember that the New Testament offers us a cosmic
Christ. We should try to read with fresh eyes that
quite astonishing first chapter of the letter to the Colos-
sians, for instance. The writer, whom many suppose

[1] From my *A Gallimaufry*.

to have been the apostle Paul himself, prays that his readers may walk worthy of the Lord unto all pleasing. This must be understood in the light of what we know of the life and teaching of Jesus, a new thing in the world. He prays that they may be fruitful in every good work and increase in the deep knowledge (the *epignosis*) of God, being fortified with all power according to God's glorious might unto all endurance and long-suffering with joy, giving thanks to God the Father, who, he says, "delivered us from the power of darkness, and hath translated us into the kingdom of his dear Son." The writer, we may observe, is reminding his readers of what is familiar to them; they all know from their own experience that they have been trans-lated out of the kingdom of darkness into the kingdom of Jesus. In him, the writer goes on, we have the for-giveness of sins; he, moreover, is the image of the in-visible God; he is the first-born of all creation, an observation which, as we may remark in passing, is com-pletely heretical from the standpoint of the later ortho-doxy. In him too the universe was created, the invisible universe no less than the visible; the universe was created both through him and unto him; he, in fact, was the Agent in all creation, as he is creation's End. In him all things consist, for it pleased God that all the divine fullness should dwell in him, and through him, through his cross, it pleased God to reconcile the whole uni-verse to himself. I do not suggest that you should ac-cept this astonishing paean as true simply because it is written in one of the books the Christians have decided to call canonical; I do not know whether it is self-consistent or even really intelligible, but here the ec-static reason, to recall that useful phrase, trying to ex-press the significance which it apprehends in the coming of Jesus Christ, calls him the image of God, the author, the redeemer, the end of the entire universe, physical and spiritual.

Now if we are thinking of the historic figure of Jesus of Nazareth, some of these words have hardly any meaning; they have little obvious connection with the Person, a man among men, depicted in the Gospels. The writer must be speaking of that of which he believes the historic Jesus to be the incarnation. I suggested before that we could naturally and properly say that Jesus of Nazareth seems to us the very incarnation of the Spirit of God. As such he might well be called God's image. We might say of him likewise that he seems to us to be the very incarnation of God's wisdom. By this we should mean that we suppose the universe to proceed from God and to find its end in God, and further, that the purpose or plan or ultimate meaning of the universe is revealed or is incarnated in the person of Jesus. That seems to me intelligible. It certainly is not obvious, but I can see, or at least I can imagine, that this is what has been apprehended by the ecstatic reason as it contemplates the life, the death, and the resurrection of Jesus Christ.

The theology of the early Church under the influence of the gospel was along these lines: Jesus was said to be God's incarnate Logos. This is a word that has no exact equivalent in English. It is much as if they had said that Jesus is the incarnate Mind of God, Purpose of God, Wisdom of God, Self-disclosure of God. There is a familiar hymn by Faber, every verse of which begins with the shocking heresy, "Jesus is God." We may observe in passing that our Roman Catholic brethren, in spite of all the advantages of a pope, are at times not preserved from surprising heresies! Jesus is not to be identified with God; the Gospels make that very plain; he trusted God, he prayed to God, not

131

to himself. To say without qualification that Jesus is God is not only heresy; it is nonsense. But it is not nonsense to suggest that if we desire to know, so far as human beings can know, the nature of God and his purposes in creation, we must set our eyes upon Jesus to the exclusion of all other figures whatsoever, especially such figures as judges or potentates or even (*pace* Sir James Jeans) mathematicians. It is not nonsense to suggest that if we would understand the purpose of history, and the purpose of the universe in that limited degree to which human beings can understand such mysteries while in *statu viatoris*, they must believe that the purposes of nature and history are consonant and compatible with the character of Jesus Christ. I am not suggesting for a moment that such a supposition could be proved. I am only saying that this has been apprehended as a revelation by the ecstatic reason of many who have contemplated the central Figure of the Gospels. It might be true. If it were true, it could be grasped only by faith and as the result of a divine self-disclosure in revelation. I claim only that such a revelation would be congruous with reason, not in contradiction to it.

It will be better not to think that we know anything about the origin and end of the universe which we can teach the scientists. Let us be content that the universe, unless it occur by chance, a supposition that seems to me merely silly and the denial of all reason, must serve a purpose, and that if God has really spoken to man, and pre-eminently in Jesus Christ, the unimaginable purpose of the cosmic process must be congruous with the little that we know. That is enough. Further I will not speculate.

But about the purpose of history we can, I think, say rather more; yet we are in the presence of great mystery. History will come to an end one day, for this planet

will not be habitable forever; and even if, as many
Americans believe, we shall before long reach the moon
(some, I believe, have their passage booked already),
the moon itself is not immortal. No, history will come
to an end, and the story will have been told. We have
no satisfactory reason for supposing that before the
end mankind will have evolved or produced an ideal
order of society which might be called in some sense
the kingdom of God. "When the Son of man cometh,
shall he find faith on the earth?" And even if one day
there should really be an ideal society, and it should
last for a thousand years (as, I remember, Hitler's empire was to last), that would not justify the unimaginable struggles, sorrows, agonies of mankind on the long
uphill way.

The purpose of history must lie beyond or outside
history. If Jesus Christ were God's Word to man, what
would this imply for the purpose of history? The question, of course, involves pre-eminently the issues of
sorrow, suffering, sin, and death. What would the redemption of history mean? Not merely that the final
chapter of the story must be happy, for the revelation
of God in Christ implies that every soul of man is dear
to God. The consummation, then, must involve not
merely the final generation but the whole process in
all its parts and in respect of every person. We have a
natural and almost ineradicable mental habit of cutting
up history into discrete events which occur and then
are over. But history is an ever-flowing process. What
my wife and I call our wedding is an event that occurred
very many years ago, but it was not really over when
all the healths had been drunk, all the cake distributed,
and the guests had all departed. What was begun then
has qualified every day of our lives since; it is the
cause of living beings whose selves are inconceivable

133

apart from it, and through their posterity may qualify the life and even be responsible for the existence of many persons yet unborn. Our wedding is an event of the past; it is also a constituent of the present; it qualifies the future. We do not know fully what anything is till we see what comes out of it in time. We think of our wedding as a good thing, but what of the bad things? In his later life Joseph spoke to his brothers about their treatment of him as a lad, when they sold him as a slave to Egypt. "You meant evil against me," said he, "but God meant it for good." (R.S.V.) For there in Egypt Joseph became prosperous, and in later days was able to save the lives of all his family, including his old father. Yet what a monstrous and unnatural crime those brothers had committed, but "where sin abounded, grace did much more abound."

Of this turning of evil to good the crucial instance in all history, as I have so often insisted, was the death of Jesus Christ in horror, in ignominy, and apparently in utter defeat. It is written of God in the Old Testament that "clouds and darkness are round about him." When Jesus died, the darkness about God was unrelieved; everything that Jesus had said, everything that men had hoped, about God seemed contradicted, and the darkness which in the story covered the whole earth for the space of three hours was a fit symbol of the darkness which hid God. Yet a few years later a writer, looking back to what had happened in those days, could declare that "God is light, and in him is no darkness at all." The cross of Christ has become for millions the symbol of victory, of hope, of reconciliation with God, the very proof of the endless love of God for all his children. From that Cross have flowed out into this disheartened and disillusioned world life-giving streams, and no man can imagine what will be the end thereof.

134

The Cross does not stand alone, but it is the supreme illustration of the redemptive activity of God made known through revelation in the bringing of good out of evil. If by revelation, by intuition, by an inward persuasion, by the ecstatic reason we have in any degree apprehended the Cross as the symbol of God's activity in history, it is permissible to suppose that the consummation, which is the fulfillment of the kingdom of God, means the similar redemption of all ills and the reconciliation of all men through the Cross beyond the veil of death. This at least would make sense of history; it is a hope, a faith, a conviction that rests upon certain palpable facts of history.

I have spoken a little, but very inconclusively, concerning Creation and Providence, the person of Christ, and the world's redemption. I may conclude with a few words about what we call the doctrine of the Trinity. I shall not say much. I have no wish to be a blind guide among the intricacies of metaphysics. But I take some exception to the phrase "the doctrine of the Trinity." There is no such thing. There are many doctrines of the Trinity; there is Augustine's, there is Abelard's, there is Leonard Hodgson's, there is Karl Barth's, and there is Paul Tillich's. Indeed, there are many more, and they differ greatly. But they all rest upon a common religious insight. This was once put to me by my friend Alec Whitehouse, of the University of Durham, in a form so clear and concise that I will but repeat his words, so far as I remember them.

We may first consider Jesus Christ in the Garden of Gethsemane praying, "Not my will, but thine, be done." That was the ultimate declaration that the Father in heaven is Lord and must be worshiped and obeyed as Lord. When we turn from the Passion to the Resurrection, we find the disciples proclaiming

135

that "God hath made that same Jesus, whom ye have crucified, both Lord and Christ." By the Resurrection Christ was exalted as Lord over all: this indeed was the earliest Christian gospel, "Believe on the Lord Jesus Christ, and thou shalt be saved." We pass from the Resurrection to Pentecost. In detail what happened then we do not know, but the matter in principle is clear. Pentecost stands for the sending of the Holy Spirit, "the Lord and Giver of life." Henceforward for the Christians the Holy Spirit is Lord of their lives. The Father is Lord, Jesus is Lord, the Spirit is Lord. Spiritually and religiously these three clauses are of identical meaning; they point to the Christian revelation, and there, so far as may be, while we are still on pilgrimage, we reach finality.